Literature about Language

In *Literature about Language* Valerie Shepherd introduces students to linguistic theory by looking at language as a theme in a variety of texts. Her emphasis is on what the texts themselves say about language. Bringing together linguistic theory and literary criticism she also looks at the ability of language to shape our perceptions, as well as the ways in which the power of language is constrained by its users and by social and cultural pressures.

Written specifically for a student audience, *Literature about Language* presumes no prior knowledge of linguistic theory, and each chapter concludes with suggestions for further work. An invaluable text for both A-Level and undergraduate students of language, literature and communication studies.

Valerie Shepherd is a lecturer in Linguistics at The Nottingham Trent University.

The INTERFACE Series

Already published:

The Series Editor

Ronald Carter is Professor of Modern English Language at the University of Nottingham and was National Co-ordinator of the 'Language in the National Curriculum' Project (LINC) from 1989 to 1992.

Literature about Language

Valerie Shepherd

London and New York

First published 1994
by Routledge
11 New Fetter Lane, London EC4P 4EE

Simultaneously published in the USA and Canada
by Routledge
29 West 35th Street, New York, NY 10001

Typeset in Times by
Ponting–Green Publishing Services, Chesham, Bucks

Printed and bound in Great Britain by
Clays Ltd, St. Ives plc
Printed on acid free paper

British Library Cataloguing in Publication Data

A catalogue record for this book is available from the
British Library.

Library of Congress Cataloging in Publication Data
Shepherd, Valerie
  Literature about language/Valerie Shepherd.
    p.   cm. – (Interface series)
  Includes bibliographical references and index.
  I. Title   II.   III. Series.

ISBN 0–415–06996–3 (hbk)
ISBN 0–415–06997–1 (pbk)

For David Fussell, who taught us
with insight and inspiration.

Contents

Series editor's introduction to the Interface series

There have been many books published this century which have been devoted to the interface of language and literary studies. This is the first series of books devoted to this area commissioned by a major international publisher; it is the first time a group of writers have addressed themselves to issues at the interface of language and literature; and it is the first time an international professional association has worked closely with a publisher to establish such a venture. It is the purpose of this general introduction to the series to outline some of the main guiding principles underlying the books in the series.

The first principle adopted is one of not foreclosing on the many possibilities for the integration of language and literature studies. There are many ways in which the study of language and literature can be combined and many different theoretical, practical and curricular objects to be realized. Obviously, a close relationship with the aims and methods of descriptive linguistics will play a prominent part, so readers will encounter some detailed analysis of language in places. In keeping with a goal of much work in this field, writers will try to make their analysis sufficiently replicable for other analysts to see how they have arrived at the interpretative decisions they have reached and to allow others to reproduce their methods on the same or on other texts. But linguistic science does not have a monopoly in methodology and description any more than linguists can have sole possession of insights into language and its workings. Some contributors to the series adopt quite rigorous linguistic procedures; others proceed less rigorously but no less revealingly. All are, however, united by a belief that detailed scrutiny of the role of language in literary texts can be mutually enriching to language and literary studies.

Series of books are usually written to an overall formula or design. In the case of the Interface series this was considered to be not entirely appropriate. This is for the reasons given above, but also because, as the first series of its kind, it would be wrong to suggest that there are formulaic modes by which integration can be achieved. The fact that all the books address themselves to the integration of language and literature in any case imparts a natural and organic unity to the series. Thus, some of the books in this series will provide descriptive overviews, others will offer detailed case studies of a particular topic, others will involve single author studies, and some will be more pedagogically oriented.

This range of design and procedure means that a wide variety of audiences is envisaged for the series as a whole, though, of course, individual books are necessarily quite specifically targeted. The general level of exposition presumes quite advanced students of language and literature. Approximately, this level covers students of English language and literature (though not exclusively English) at senior high-school/upper sixth-form level to university students in their first or second year of study. Many of the books in the series are designed to be used by students. Some may serve as course books – these will normally contain exercises and suggestions for further work as well as glossaries and graded bibliographies which point the student towards further reading. Some books are also designed to be used by teachers for their own reading and updating, and to supplement courses; in some cases, specific questions of pedagogic theory, teaching procedure and methodology at the interface of language and literature are addressed.

From a pedagogic point of view it is the case in many parts of the world that students focus on literary texts, especially in the mother tongue, before undertaking any formal study of the language. With this fact in mind, contributors to the series have attempted to gloss all new technical terms and to assume on the part of their readers little or no previous knowledge of linguistics or formal language studies. They see no merit in not being detailed and explicit about what they describe in the linguistic properties of texts; but they recognize that formal language study can seem forbidding if it is not properly introduced.

A further characteristic of the series is that the authors engage in a direct relationship with their readers. The overall style of writing is informal and there is above all an attempt to lighten the usual style of academic discourse. In some cases this extends to the way in which notes and guidance for further work are presented. In all cases, the style adopted by authors is judged to be that most appropriate to the mediation of their chosen subject matter.

We now come to two major points of principle which underlie the conceptual scheme for the series. One is that the term 'literature' cannot be defined in isolation from an expression of ideology. In fact, no academic study, and certainly no description of the language of texts, can be neutral and objective, for the sociocultural positioning of the analyst will mean that the description is unavoidably political. Contributors to the series recognize and, in so far as this accords with the aims of each book, attempt to explore the role of ideology at the interface of language and literature. Second, most writers also prefer the term 'literatures' to a singular notion of literature. Some replace 'literature' altogether with the neutral term 'text'. It is for this reason that readers will not find exclusive discussions of the literary language of canonical literary texts; instead the linguistic heterogeneity of literature and the permeation of many discourses with what is conventionally thought of as poetic or literary language will be a focus. This means that in places as much space can be devoted to examples of word play in jokes, newspaper editorials, advertisements, historical writing, or a popular thriller as to a sonnet by Shakespeare or a passage from Jane Austen. It is also important to stress how the term 'literature' itself is historically variable and how different social and cultural assumptions can condition what is regarded as literature. In this respect the role of linguistic and literary theory is vital. It is an aim of the series to be constantly alert to new developments in the description and theory of texts.

Finally, as series editor, I have to underline the partnership and co-operation of the whole enterprise of the Interface series and acknowledge the advice and assistance received at many stages from the PALA Committee and from Routledge. In turn, we are all fortunate to have the benefit of three associate editors with considerable collective depth of experience in this field in different parts of the world: Professor Roger Fowler, Professor Mary Louise Pratt, Professor Michael Halliday. In spite of their own individual orientations, I am sure that all concerned with the series would want to endorse the statement by Roman Jakobson made over twenty-five years ago but which is no less relevant today:

> A linguist deaf to the poetic function of language and a literary scholar indifferent to linguistic problems and unconversant with linguistic methods, are equally flagrant anachronisms.

Valerie Shepherd's contribution to the *Interface* series is an original and distinctive one. The relationship between linguistics and literature is usually conceived of as unilinear, insights from linguistics being deployed to illuminate the nature of literary texts or serving as a descriptive base from which interpretations can be constructed. In *Literature About Language* Dr Shepherd turns this relationship inside out by looking at literary texts for the insights they provide into the nature of language and for the ways in which language itself is construed as a topic or theme for literary exploration. By seeing language as subject, much is learned not only about the literary medium but about how reflections on and self-consciousness about language are an essential part of the meaning-making process in a wide range of texts and genres. *Literature About Language* is a significant contribution to explorations at the interface of literary and linguistic studies.

Acknowledgements

I am grateful to all those, including John Tomlinson, David Woods, Paul Doust and Nick Shepherd who gave me advice in the preparation of this book and to colleagues Elizabeth Morrish and Sheila Hermolle, who helped me find time to write. Special thanks are due to David Fussell for his endless patience and support.

Acknowledgement is due to Centaur Press Ltd and the editor Bernard Jones for extracts from *The Poems of William Barnes*, 1962, and to Tom Leonard for permission to reprint 'right inuff ma language is disgraceful' from *Intimate Voices: 1965–1983*, Galloping Dog Press, 1984, and 'and their judges spoke with one dialect' from *Situations Theoretical and Contemporary* Galloping Dog Press, 1986.

Jonathan Swift's poem 'The furniture of a woman's mind' is reprinted by permission of Oxford University Press from *The Poems of Jonathan Swift*, ed. Harold Williams, 1958.

'Nervous prostration' by Anna Wickham is reprinted with permission of Virago Press from *The Writings of Anna Wickham*, ed. R. D. Smith, published by Virago Press 1984 copyright © James and George Hepburn *The Man With The Hammer* (1916).

Introduction
Literature about language

Each chapter in *Literature about Language* concerns literary texts which refer, among their themes, to some aspect of language and language use. The chapter discusses this aspect in terms of linguistic theory and then relates the discussion to a critique of the texts. Suggestions for further work follow each chapter. (A list of chapters and their topics is given at the end of this introduction.)

However, although each of the chapters concentrates on a different area of language and linguistic theory, all of them are concerned with two major tenets: (a) the immensely powerful creativity of language; and (b) the constraints that limit that human creativity.

Chapter 1 argues that William Golding's *The Inheritors* (1955) is essentially about this creative ability. In Golding's novel it is a force which is a key to survival, both for Golding's fictitious 'inheritors' and – chapter 1 and the rest of *Literature about Language* suggest – for ourselves. However, *The Inheritors* also exemplifies the limitations which are the second main concern of this book. For instance, Lok and his fellows, 'the people' who inhabit the world at the beginning of Golding's novel, do have language. That is, they have vocabulary and syntax. But the uses to which they put their linguistic capacity are unsophisticated. In consequence, their ability to survive – unlike that of the invading 'inheritors' – is tragically limited. It is true that Lok and the people's ineffective use of language power is not only the result of limited skills and techniques: it is also partly a result of their very narrow experience of the world. For the invaders and their way of life is so alien to anything the people have known that, in order to grasp and express what is happening to them, Lok and his tribe cannot perceptively structure their syntax, or find appropriate words in their limited lexicon, or create new ones. Nevertheless, in addition, these original people are significantly deficient in the *art* of language.

To begin with, they are not accomplished in the art of *narration*. And it is, I suggest, partly for this reason that Lok and his fellows do not survive. By contrast, the talent for narration is amply possessed by the inheriting tribe – and by ourselves. Our powerful capacity for perceptive, life-constructing narration is the subject of chapter 5, which discusses Elizabeth Jennings' poetry (1989), and also James Joyce's short story, 'Eveline' (in Joyce 1977). This chapter is particularly concerned with the syntactic choices that are made by the creators of everyday, personal narratives (as well as by literary artists) in order to 'label' and to assess the roles and relationships they perceive in the unfolding of their tale. These selections are discussed in relation to aspects of Halliday's systemic grammar, and to models of narrative described by Labov and by Greimas. It would appear that the power and importance of such choices, within the narrative form, cannot be overestimated, given the psychologist Sarbin's argument that 'survival in a world of meanings is problematic without the talent to make up and to interpret stories about interweaving lives' (1986: 11). But in Lok and the people the ability to tell stories, to use the structure of a tale to give order and explanation to remembered experiences, is only rudimentary. In consequence, they are less able than the inheriting Tuami and his tribe to comprehend and learn from their past. Nor can Lok, Ha and the others readily use the story form as a heuristic device to assess and plan for possible futures: they cannot imagine and order a chronology of likely events, hypothesizing their probable causal links and results. Moreover, they are quite unable to adjust their perception of the present in order to take account of the inheritors' arrival in their world. But we – modern, competent narrators – practise what Robinson and Hawpe (1986) call 'narrative repair'. For us, as they explain (1986: 123), 'interpretive perspectives change prompting reevaluation of . . . the original account' we had made of our experiences. Lok and his fellows, however, cannot 'language' a new story, cannot encompass new sensations, people and events. They cannot repair their view of the world in order to comprehend – and survive – their changing circumstances.

Moreover, Lok and the people's capacity to use language imaginatively, working through it to reach out from existing knowledge to discover new and increased understanding, is drastically limited in other ways. Of course it is true that Lok does, in a sudden 'convulsion of understanding' (Golding 1961: 194), realize that he can make *similes*. He perceives that his experiences are sometimes *like* others he has had and his language expresses and draws attention to their similarity, helping him to extend his understanding of a feeling, an object, event, or idea in terms of what he knows about another. This language creativity could help him to achieve some understanding of the inheritors. It 'could grasp the white-faced hunters with a hand, could put them into the world where they were thinkable and not a random and unrelated irruption' (Golding 1961: 194). But the imaginative linguistic power of comparison comes too late to give Lok sufficient comprehension of his changing circumstances. Tuami and his fellows, on the other hand, have command of simile. They can, moreover, extend simile to metaphor, a creative manoeuvre of language and thought which Lok rarely achieves but which we – twentieth-century inheritors of the world – use with subtlety and proficiency.

Indeed, in a very real sense – as chapter 4, concerning Susan Sontag's *AIDS and its Metaphors* (1988), and the poem 'Time out' by Eva Salzman (Rumens 1992: 62), discusses – we depend upon metaphor. For what Lakoff and Johnson (1980) call its 'imaginative rationality' is, as they explain, crucial to our understanding. They argue that 'our ordinary conceptual system, in terms of which we both think and act, is fundamentally metaphorical in nature' (1980: 3). However, our dependence is not without danger. For metaphors, by definition, reveal only partial truths. They must highlight certain aspects of meaning in the comparisons they draw whilst leaving others in shadow. (If we call someone an angel we do not, surely, imply they have halo and wings in addition to their 'angelic' qualities of, say, goodness and kindness which we are presumably wishing to emphasize through the metaphor.) In consequence, inferences may be made which are damaging. For instance, Sontag is critical of describing AIDS in terms of 'stages': first, the stage of infection with HIV, then ARC, then AIDS. She objects because, she says, to speak of staging implies unavoidable progression, from one step to another. It assumes and concentrates on the inevitability of AIDS following HIV infection. Thus it can, by directing thinking towards death, reduce the quality of life while it is lived. For it may shift the focus from the present, both for those who are HIV positive and for those who control these people's jobs, or financial affairs, or who are involved in personal relationships with them. The implication of Sontag's argument is that we must scrutinize the metaphors we encounter, recognize their partialness and, bearing their inevitable 'blind spots' in mind, use them more carefully.

But this is no easy matter. Not only is it made difficult by the nature of metaphor itself, ignoring, as it must, some portion of a comparison's meaning; in addition, metaphor's inevitable partialness may be perfectly acceptable to its users. For example, Golding's inheriting Tuami finds strength in a metaphor that helps him come to terms with a relationship and with the prospect of his future. But the metaphor, naturally, leaves in shadow certain complexities and difficulties. Yet it is doubtful

whether Tuami could have coped with an awareness of these complications at the moment he conceived, and was sustained by, the metaphor.

Moreover, what is true of metaphor is true of all kinds of language:
the use of language is made complex by its very nature and it is, besides,
subject to the power, and the weakness, of its human users.

Chapter 2, for example, considers the immense expressive, communicative potential that is available to human beings through choices
from the rules, systems and structures that are the defining features of
language. We are dependent upon these aspects of language – but it is
this very dependence which gives us the independence and freedom to
say what we will. This argument is supported here through examples of
everyday uses of language and, also, more unusual feminist and
Rastafarian linguistic manoeuvres. Yet we do not always exploit the
tremendous creativity of our language resource. The reasons for
restraint or repression are numerous, just as, the chapter argues,
characters in the e. e. cummings poem, 'my sweet old etcetera'
(Firmage 1981: 275), seem prevented from fully utilizing their linguistic capacity for a variety of reasons that could be emotional,
psychological, social, experimental or intellectual.

Besides, not only may language users limit their communicative
potential but also listeners (and readers) do not always – through
inability or through disinclination – acknowledge the messages they
hear. For one thing, the systems of language are intricate and subtle in
their signalling of meaning. The point is made, with specific regard to
phonological systems, in Thomas Hardy's poem 'The upper birch-
leaves' (Gibson 1976: 507), discussed in chapter 3. Hardy's choices of
sound and rhythm actually demonstrate the difficulty. For the poem's
reader–hearer may, literally, be deaf to fine yet significant differences
of vowels and consonants, rhymes, rhythms and intonational patterns.
In consequence we may not at first, until encouraged to do so in the
second half of the poem, recognize their potential for meaning.

Furthermore, the intimations of mortality carried by the poem's
sounds are not necessarily welcome: we may prefer not to listen and
choose instead to turn a deliberately deaf ear. Our power to ignore the
language of others – and in effect to silence them – is also at issue in
Anna Wickham's 'Nervous prostration' (Smith 1984: 210). Her poem,
discussed in chapter 7, deals with difficulties of communication
between men and women. These difficulties appear to stem, in part,
from the different ways in which language may be used by men and by
women and, most importantly, from the different values attached to
these contrasts and their meanings.

Actually, there were differences between the methods of communication valued by men and by women even amongst Golding's Lok and the people. The people believed that men had the skill of thought and reason: they 'pictured'. But women's power was spiritual and, therefore, of greater value, or so it seemed to Lok: 'As long as there was a woman there was life. But what use was a man save for smelling things out and having pictures?' (Golding 1961: 85). Yet Lok's self-deprecation, and his veneration for women and for their kind of communication, has not, traditionally, been shared by men in the modern world. Swift's 'The furniture of a woman's mind' (Williams 1958: 415–18) mocks women's language, its form and its content. It is perceived by this poem's persona as sets of 'phrases learnt by rote' and illogical, scandal-mongering tittle-tattle. By implication, chapter 7 argues, the poem admires men for using a very different, apparently weighty and logical, form of language. And yet, before the inheritors finally defeated the people, it was Fa, the woman, who not only was the more spiritual but also made 'better' – in the sense of more effectively 'thoughtful' – use of language than Lok. But then, a male-biased view seems to have persistently distorted evaluation of any example of women's language, at least for Swift and those of his persuasion. Certainly, the 'man from the Croydon class', described in Wickham's poem, hears in his wife's talk – irrationally in her estimation – something that 'vexes' him. Whatever it is, he does not respond to her and so, in effect, her language is silenced, to the extent that, instead of talking, she feels she must 'sob or shriek' in order to force her husband to 'live, or to love' or even 'to speak'.

It is perhaps no wonder that Wickham's persona suffers from such 'nervous prostration'. For it can be argued that language is tantamount to identify, so that to be unheard is to be nullified. The relationship between language and a sense of self, and a sense of place and community, is also the subject of chapter 6. It considers Non-standard varieties of English through the dialect poetry of Barnes, Tennyson and Leonard, and in relation to present-day government directives for language teaching.

William Barnes believed that, by writing in the sounds, words and syntax of the nineteenth-century Blackmore Vale, he was giving its people a 'poetry of their own' (Barnes 1841: 510–11). Those families who spoke the language evidently agreed, eagerly packing to capacity the halls and houses in which Barnes gave readings of his work. Their pleasure was not surprising, for Gerard Manley Hopkins thought it was 'as if Dorset life and Dorset landscape had taken flesh and tongue' in the poems (Abbott 1955: 220–2) and Barnes' daughter observed that 'it was the first time a Dorset audience had heard its feelings, language, and daily life portrayed in its own common speech' (Scott 1887: 167). But of course, the rarity of Non-standard dialect poetry is unsurprising, given a traditional conviction that only the Standard is 'correct'. Non-standard varieties of English – and by implication their speakers – have long been rejected as incorrect and unexpressive. But the chapter refutes arguments of this kind by demonstrating the rule-based, creative and communicative power of Non-standard dialects. It accepts, nevertheless, Sir John Kingman's pragmatic view (expressed in his *Report of the Committee of Inquiry into the Teaching of English* (1988) that, given Standard English's widespread power and endorsement, all children in this country have a 'right' (Kingham 1988: 14) to be taught this variety. At the same time, however, the Kingman report urged that any child's Non-standard English should be respected, not only for its communicative strengths but also as a highly expressive mark of his or her family and community identity: the Standard should merely be added to the child's repertoire and certainly not enforced as a replacement. Moreover, the report recommended that language teaching should go far beyond instruction in vocabulary and syntax. It should, for example, include consideration of all language users' potential – whether they choose a Standard or Non-standard variety of language – for stylistic choice and for varied and powerful discourse patterns in relation to different social and cultural contexts. Explicit knowledge of this kind can increase control over, and sensitivity to, language. At the same time it should modify unthinking hostility to the Non-standard and encourage its acceptance as a legitimate and respected alternative voice.

Government directives for the teaching of English followed in the spirit of the Kingman report. Nevertheless, during the latter stages of this book's preparation, National Curriculum requirements for the teaching of English in England and Wales have been reviewed and policy is to change again, this time towards increased emphasis on the use of Standard English – not only in the classroom, but also in the playground. However, whilst there is pragmatism in the teaching of the Standard, it will be unfortunate if other varieties are, in consequence, rejected as incorrect and unexpressive. There is an Arab proverb (of which William Barnes approved): 'A man by learning a second language becomes two' – and in some ways a dialect is a second language. Conversely, if we do not listen carefully to another's variety of language we do not fully understand that speaker. The same is true of the written word.

For example, William Golding's Lok was, tragically, under the misapprehension that he and his fellows have only to exchange words with the newcomers and in consequence rapport will be achieved. He insisted, 'People understand each other' (Golding 1961: 71–2). But the inheritors did not understand Lok, any more than Lok comprehended them. Similarly, in our inherited world, people speaking different languages may perceive experience in different ways, in part because of their language's contrasting lexicon and structures (as the Sapir–Whorf hypothesis, discussed in chapters 1 and 4 suggests). But even people who speak the same language variety, selecting from the same options of syntax and lexicon, frequently do not hear one another clearly. For, cutting across all variations of this kind, there is also variation at the level of discourse (in the sense of the word as it is used in chapter 8). The linguist Wilhelm von Humboldt (1767–1835) described human beings as trapped in circles of language, and his metaphor may be extended to discourses. If we cannot step into another person's circle – of language, dialect or discourse – we cannot meet them on their own terms.

This difficulty is one of the themes of David Lodge's novel *Nice Work* (1989), which is discussed in chapter 8 with reference to work on the language of the law courts by Sandra Harris (for example 1984, 1988, 1989) and poetry by Tom Leonard (1986). Lodge's protagonists – an engineering works manager, Vic Wilcox, and an academic, Robyn Penrose – share English but, in effect, speak very different languages. For Vic lives by the discourses of profit and loss – and of romantic love. Robyn rejects these, particularly the language of romance as – like all discourses, to her way of thinking – a kind of fiction, a construction placed on social contexts and behaviour by language and its users, users who are themselves shaped by the language they have spoken or written. Robyn prefers her own discourses of, for example, feminism, discourses whose underlying ideologies are generally in direct opposition to those within which Vic lives his life. Given some deliberate effort, each comes to understand something of the other's point of view and even to adapt their habitual discourses accordingly. But their differences cannot always comfortably co-exist or be adjusted to mutual satisfaction. Ultimately, it is cultural, social and personal powers aside from language itself which (as discussed by Harris and exemplified in poetry by Leonard) determine whose will be the louder – in the sense of more effective and controlling – voice.

In sum then, the rules and elements of language, and the human art of language use are, as the defeat of Lok and the survival of the inheritors demonstrate, immensely powerful. But these are complex powers which we may not – as the discussion of cummings' poem and also of narrative structuring argue – always utilize to full capacity. Moreover, as the chapters on Hardy's poem and on Sontag's essay exemplify, we need a fine sensitivity to their subtleties if we are to respond fully to the words and structures of others. Besides, communication is not merely a matter of skilful language practice, heard by a sensitive ear. Social and cultural factors affect the vitality and power of our linguistic inheritance, controlling – as the chapters on Non-standard English, on women's use of language and on discourse demonstrate – the communicative power which is possessed by all human beings.

Literature about Language's final chapter draws together these two themes – first, the powerful creativity of language and, second, the constraints upon it – which have been in mind throughout the book. It does so in relation to Nadine Gordimer's short story, 'Something for the time being' (1983). The story is, in part, about the signalling of meanings, meanings that reside in a multiplicity of signs (including icons, indexes and the arbitrary symbols of human language) all of which are shaped, and linked together in significant structures, by their human creators, their interpreters, and by the social forces which press upon all users of language. It is about success – and about failure – in this signalling.

Two further examples of literature about language (not discussed elsewhere in this book) encapsulate these tensions that exist between understanding and misunderstanding, and also between language power and language constraints.

First, a poem by Emily Dickinson images meaning as 'freight', a cargo that is carried within the words and structures of language. But this freight is 'undeveloped'. For there is, as *Literature about Language* argues, profound limitation and weakness in human language use. That is, we do not say all there is to say. We do not understand all that is said. We are unaware of all that lies behind the utterances we make and hear. Indeed,

> Could mortal lip divine
> The undeveloped freight
> Of a developed syllable
> 'Twould crumble with the weight.
> > (Johnson 1976: 602)

Literature about Language argues, as this Introduction explains, that language and its users cannot bear the full weight of meaning – its 'undeveloped freight' – partly because of the nature of language itself and partly because of the social, cultural and psychological pressures upon those who speak and write.

Even so, the human power of language, as a means of creative thinking and also of manipulation, is immense and not to be underestimated. And so, secondly, as Dickinson writes in another poem, although an utterance may seem innocuous, a 'quiet' thing, it can, nevertheless, be the fuse which lights a fire: it can be the vital spark to hitherto unrealized meanings. As she says,

> A Man may make a Remark –
> In itself – a quiet thing
> That may furnish the Fuse unto a Spark
> In dormant nature – lain
>   (Johnson 1983: vol. 2, p. 691)

Literature about Language describes some of this tremendous potential and its consequences. But, at the same time, it acknowledges that the potency of language lies in materials so familiar to us, and so often used unthinkingly, that we may underestimate their power and our skill. Therefore, as Dickinson urges – and in order to preserve our inheritance –

> Let us deport – with skill –
> Let us discourse – with care –
> Powder exists in Charcoal –
> Before it exists in Fire.
>   (Johnson 1975: 446)

ORDER OF CHAPTERS

The chapters of *Literature about Language* are organized as follows. Chapter 1 introduces the book's themes through a consideration of William Golding's *The Inheritors*. Chapters 2 and 3 describe some of the elements of language and their vast, though frequently constrained, potential for creative use. Chapters 4 and 5 look at the deployment of these creative resources through metaphor (chapter 4) and through narrative (chapter 5). Chapters 6 and 7 discuss the power of language in relation to social and cultural contexts: chapter 6 is concerned with attitudes to class and language, whilst chapter 7 considers the politics of gender and language. Chapters 8 and 9 draw together the book's themes of power and constraint, acknowledging the immense capacity of language to construct and to convey meaning but, at the same time, emphasizing the restrictions placed upon it by its human users or their hearers.

Suggestions for further work, relating to the language of literature and, alternatively, to language in everyday use, follow each chapter.

1 The human capacity for language
The Inheritors by William Golding

In William Golding's novel, The Inheritors *(1955), Lok and his companions are ancient hominids who die out. They are survived by others whose far more complex language capacity helps them to inherit the world. It is a language capacity which, in its sophistication, resembles our own linguistic power. In consequence, the novel gives the reader insight into the language ability that, in a very real sense, makes us human and has allowed us to survive. Conversely, discussion of our linguistic capacity may throw light on the novel.*

However, whilst The Inheritors's *imaginative speculation is revealing with regard to the nature and functions of language as we know it, the novel is not of course an historical account of the origins of language. (These in any case remain unclear.[1])*

The following chapter introduces aspects of language and language use including:

arbitrariness
semanticity
structure dependence
creativity
displacement
linguistic determinism and cultural relativity
simile and metaphor
narrative structuring
transitivity

Subsequent chapters build on this one, returning to these matters in greater detail.

All page references are to the 1961 edition of the novel, which was first published in 1955.

THE SURVIVAL OF THE FITTEST

The Inheritors is obviously not a history book. True, given the quotation from H.G. Wells which appears after the title page, it seems to be a reaction to Wells' *Outline of History* (1920), disputing his vision of a repulsive, cannibalistic Neanderthal and replacing it with the gentler Lok. Moreover, compared with fossil records, Lok certainly looks much as Neanderthal man really did appear: Golding writes that his 'square hands swung down to the knees . . . head . . . slightly forward on the strong neck . . . mouth. . . wide and soft . . . and above the upper lip the great nostrils . . . flared like wings' (219). It is also true that the inheriting Tuami and his fellows – thinner, taller and more upright than the Neanderthal, with forehead lower than Lok's and nose more prominent (138–44) – do resemble Cro-Magnon Man, a species to whom Neanderthals did, in actuality, give way about 30,000 years ago. But here historical likelihood stops, and the more imaginative speculation of art takes over.

For one thing, Lok's language is much more distinct than a true Neanderthal's oral expression could have been. Computer-modelling research (Lieberman 1984) has demonstrated that a Neanderthal would have sounded slow, nasal and indistinct, lacking most vowel sounds and many consonants, especially [k] and [g]. And though Cro-Magnon speech was in reality much more developed, given a vocal tract that was better adapted for talk than the Neanderthal's, it is unlikely to have taken the precise form of Tuami's English – which of course Golding needed in order to communicate his ideas to twentieth-century readers!

Yet, although Lok and Tuami's speech forms are necessarily inaccurate in an anthropological sense, we are nevertheless offered, through their carefully constructed and finely tuned imaginative representation, an insight into the human condition. We are not exactly reading a version of historical fact, but comparing Lok's language with that of the inheriting newcomers goes some way towards *accounting for* our history.

That is, the book would seem to be a comment upon evolution, to be about the survival of the fittest. And it relates fitness to the kind of language capacity that Tuami and the new people had evolved, a capacity in some senses way beyond the kind possessed by Lok and his fellows. Moreover, the linguistic power of the new people appears in certain important respects to be much as ours is today. To this extent we can see something of ourselves in *The Inheritors*. Its imaginative contrast and comparison between two sorts of language (which we hear not only in the dialogue of the two peoples, but also in the narrating voice that for chapters 1–11 sometimes echoes Lok's language but, in chapter 12, seems to speak for Tuami) is a comment on the linguistic capability that we, as modern inheritors – survivors – do actually possess. Indeed, it is a comment on *what makes us human*.

LANGUAGE AND 'HUMANNESS'

In a sense it is language that makes us human. Though animals have their own, often intricate and sophisticated communication systems, they do not have our language. Therefore they are different from ourselves – not human. Lok and the people are different from other creatures that inhabit their world because, unlike the hyenas and ravens, they have what we call language. They are thus, by the language definition, human – but only, I shall argue, in a limited way.

What we define as language – whether it be an ancient form, or modern-day English, or Japanese, or Swahili, or whatever – has certain characteristics. The linguist, Charles Hockett, listed sixteen of these 'design features' (see Hockett and Altmann 1968) and a number of similar ones are described in detail by Jean Aitchison in *The Articulate Mammal* (1989: 25–33). These include *arbitrariness*, *semanticity*, *structure dependence* and *displacement*, all of which are briefly discussed below. Use of the vocal–auditory channel, however, is not an indispensable feature: the signing of those whose hearing is impaired shares with speech the all-important defining characteristics of language.

Taken together, these design features allow us tremendous linguistic flexibility and creativity. Some, as Aitchison explains, are possessed by certain animals, but only to a limited degree and no animal has all of them.

First, the words of language are generally *arbitrary*. That is, they rarely feel in the mouth, sound to the ear, remotely like that which they signify: they can sound like more or less anything at all. So we English speakers refer to a four-legged creature that barks as a *dog*, but the French have chosen the equally arbitrary label, *chien*, and the Germans, *Hund*. True, Lok remembers the sound made by the ravens and, flapping at them with his arms, shouts 'Kwak' (25), imitating the memory and seeming to name them onomatopoeically. But, like modern-day speakers, he does not use many words of the non-arbitrary kind. (Whilst the general arbitrary principle still holds good, some languages, notably Japanese, do have a larger proportion of onomatopoeic words than Indo-European languages.)

Because a word is usually arbitrary in this way, with no clue to its significance in its sound, users must more or less agree on and remember what it means to them. And words have relatively precise meanings: that is, they have *semanticity*. This takes them a long way from the very approximate meanings of animal whimpers and growls, grunts and roars. Of course, humans make such screams and groans too, in response to pain, fear, pleasure and so on. But we can also be much more specific: we can say, for instance, whether our pain is a headache, a hangover, a migraine or whatever and English speakers, knowing the meanings of these words, will know which pills and potions and how much sympathy to dole out. Moreover, our choice of word is comparatively voluntary, unlike the involuntary groan or cry. (It may be that some animals have similar semantic precision. When the vervet monkey sees a reptile it makes a 'chutter' sound. Perhaps this means 'snake', because the monkey makes different noises in the presence of different kinds of danger. However, the animal's vocabulary would seem to be minute and, besides, it may still be that the sounds are involuntary indications of fear, altering only in relation to the degree of danger and not labelling the stimuli themselves.)

Nil, one of the original people in *The Inheritors*, uses a lot of animal-like cries: she has a habit of moaning gently when tired and hungry, and when struggling to cross a log she calls out 'ai, ai' (14, 18). But, in the main, Nil, Lok and the rest of the people have moved on beyond animals to include in their communication, as we do, arbitrary signs, used for specific meanings.

However, words become even more communicative, their potential to mean increased, when they are placed in a structure. Language users come to know, without formal teaching, the particular *rules of structuring* practised by their language community. These 'rules' are not inhibiting in any way. On the contrary, as the American linguist Noam Chomsky has pointed out (1957), given a vocabulary and rules for putting these words together, human beings are infinitely creative. We do not merely parrot utterances that we have heard before. In English, word order is a very important way of structuring. So *The grubs bit Lok* means something quite different from *Lok bit the grubs*: a very simple structural change totally alters meaning. Similarly, *Fa calls Lok* means something different from *Fa called Lok*: differences of tense, in English, may be signalled by differences in the internal structure of verbs. Other languages may manipulate structure in different ways, but all use it to convey meaning.

On the other hand, experiments with chimpanzees have shown that, although they may be taught some language design features, they do not, despite being relatively intelligent animals, grasp rules of structuring. It would seem, therefore, that there is something *innate* in the human capacity for language which, given a language environment, develops naturally, without formal teaching (see Aitchison 1989).

Moreover, once words and the rules of structuring these words meaningfully and creatively are acquired, language users have a particular freedom not possessed by most animals. We can – unlike animals whose involuntary signals are generally a *part* of their present feeling of pain, or hunger, or danger – choose to communicate about things and ideas and events which are not in our immediate environment. We have, that is, a feature of language called *displacement*. Bees have some displacement for, using a 'vocabulary' of dance movements, they are able to report back to the hive the location and quantity of food they have discovered some distance away. However, their limited 'vocabulary' of movements restricts them to directions and the amount of available food: they cannot give their opinion of the new queen bee or the state of next door's garden. In our case, however, displacement helps us to recall the past, invent the future, write imaginative art – and, of course, tell lies.

Lok certainly has displacement. It even accounts for one of his most charming qualities. For Lok tells lies, not destructive and damaging lies but the white lies of fantasizing children. 'I shall' he declares 'bring back food in my arms . . . so much food that I stagger . . . a deer . . . under this left arm . . . under this right one . . . the quarters of a cow' (37–9). Fa grins and tells him there is not so much food in the world.

In sum, then, Lok and his fellows do have language: arbitrary signifiers, semanticity, rules of structure, displacement, all these things allowing for voluntary, creative communication. In this sense they have humanness.

However, as far as language goes, the people have humanness only to a very limited degree. For the *uses* to which they put their language capacity are (as I shall argue below and in subsequent chapters) far less powerful than those that we – and Tuami and the newcomers – employ. That is, the language of Lok and the people is functionally weak in certain vital ways. For instance, there is little in the way of metaphor, little in the way of logic, little in the way of complex story-telling. In short, there is little *directed thinking*.

Of course, not all thought depends upon language. Emotional responses, day-dreams, routine operations like following the route to work, do not seem to require language.

Besides, we do not use language purely for thinking and to communicate ideas. Many cultures (though others, like the Paliyans of southern India, are quite comfortable with silence) also use it to maintain rapport between people. Utterances like *Good morning!* and *How are you?* do not carry weighty thoughts and do not require a detailed, thoughtful weather report or medical prognosis in return. Malinowski, the anthropologist (1884–1942), called these sorts of exchange *phatic communion*. Lok seems to be enjoying something similar when he talks to the people 'generally, laughing, hearing only words from his mouth but wanting laughter' (15).

Yet the people are not without directed thought of any kind. They refelect upon what they term 'pictures', but the process is clearly an effort. Fa says,

'I am by the sea and I have a picture. This is a picture of a picture. I am –' She screwed up her face and scowled – 'thinking'.

(62)

It is the *explanation of* thoughts, sorting them out, reasoning from them and building upon them, that seems to be the difficulty. Once, Fa followed a scent 'without reason. She knew the fire must be at the other end but to say why, she would have had to stop and wrestle with pictures, holding her hands to her head' (127). Yet, in her kind of life, constantly striving to find food, keep warm, ensure safety from hyenas, there is little time or energy for such wondering, for reasoning.

But pressures of life are not the only obstacles that restrict the people's reasoning power. Besides, though vastly different, their existence is not necessarily more pressured than our modern condition, yet for us language is clearly a supreme power. However, there is another difficulty, a difficulty which relates to the *Sapir–Whorf hypothesis*. It is a problem which we encounter but which seems to inhibit Lok and the people even more than ourselves.

LINGUISTIC DETERMINISM AND CULTURAL RELATIVITY: THE SAPIR–WHORF HYPOTHESIS

Fa imagines how much more convenient it would be if a plant that she and Lok are eating could grow nearer to their home. She puts her hands wide apart, evidently signifying the distance between the two places, home by the fall and the clearing where the two of them now sit companionably munching. Then she brings her hands together and in so doing seems to consider moving the plant to the other area, closer to home. If this is Fa's intention she could be groping towards the concept of cultivation. However, though she has a picture, a thought, Fa has no words to develop what it might mean: 'though the tilt of her head, the eyebrows moved slightly up and apart asked a question she had no words with which to define it' (49).

The difficulty here is partly one of inadequate vocabulary, the lexicon not having caught up with awareness. Lok encountered the same problem on the day when, for the first time, he saw 'the other'. For him it was a day of 'total newness' (114). There were, for example, new smells. One came from 'a peculiarly thick and fiery sort of mud that his nose could identify as different but not name' (181). Worse, having encountered 'the other', Lok felt 'cut off and no longer one of the people . . . [but he] had no words to formulate these thoughts' (78).

His plight recalls the Sapir–Whorf hypothesis developed by the anthropologist and linguist Edward Sapir (1884–1939) and his student Benjamin Lee Whorf (1897–1941). The hypothesis is about linguistic determinism and cultural relativity. At its most extreme it suggests that our perception of the world is largely *determined* for us by the particular language we acquire along with our speech community. Whorf argued that 'the world is presented in a kaleidoscopic flux of impressions which has to be organized by our minds – and this means largely by the linguistic systems of our minds' (Carroll and Wiley 1956: 213). To put it crudely, if our language does not have a word for something then that something does not exist for us.

Yet, formulated this way, the hypothesis is overstated. After all, though Lok had no word for the new smell, he had not failed to notice it. And his separation from the people was felt if not 'languaged'. As for ourselves, we function adequately in a technological age even when we cannot label all the parts of the machines we operate.

The difficulty, however, is that, lacking relevant language (like Lok in his loneliness and Fa when she is groping towards an understanding of cultivation), we may be limited in giving full shape and significance to an idea and, if this is the case, we shall certainly not be able to communicate it efficiently.

Still, it is possible that we can invent the necessary language. For, as we mentioned earlier, being human means, in part, having the capacity for infinite linguistic creativity. As Sapir himself remarked, 'aborigines that had never seen or heard of a horse were compelled to invent or borrow a word for the animal when they made his acquaintance' (1921: 219). Present-day examples would be our invention of new terms to match new technology (*wordprocessor*, *hypertext*), new perceptions (*Ms*, *chairperson*) or new knowledge (*genes*, though always in existence in some sense, have only recently been identified and labelled as part of a modern theory of biology). Not that we are always swift to create and change. With increasing feminist awareness, many English speakers are now troubled by the lack of a 'catch-all' pronoun to cover both genders. Having only *he* and *she* to choose from, we so often give the impression, by selecting *he* when both sexes are involved, that the female population is excluded. The sentence, *Man walked upright from the forest and acquired language*, might imply by default that women scuttled silently along behind. But, instead of creating a new, third term we may try a kind of circumlocution: *she/he (or s/he) emerged from the trees, and his/her capacity for language developed*. However, this is cumbersome and *s/he* only works in writing. Besides, an indication of the presence but also the *separateness* of the two genders may not be quite what we intend on every occasion. *They* might do in plural cases of this nature, but could be taken to mean men only. As for the singular, those who would like to imply a blended, fused combination of male and female characteristics in, for example, God have no pronoun at all with which to do so in English. (This has not been the case in every language. Aztec described its god as having both male and female characteristics, referred to him/her as *ometeotl* 'two god', but followed this plural concept with singular verb forms. The relevant pronoun was *yejua* which signified 'he, she, or it' (Key 1975: 20).)

Furthermore, even if something is recognized – be it a new object, a feeling or an idea – we may, without labelling it and storing its label in the language for future use, be slow to notice that something on subsequent occasions. When snow halted railways and plunged the country into darkness in 1991, officials were heard to say they were unprepared because 'it was the wrong kind of snow'. Would the snow ploughs and emergency generators have been at the ready if only English had words that label not merely 'snow' but many different kinds of these ice-crystals? Experiments have certainly shown greater ease in memorizing objects and concepts if a language contains convenient labels (see Landar, Ervin and Horowitz 1960). As for Lok and the people, would they have followed the sick Mal too early from their winter quarters if their language had been more comprehensive, if it had been ready with words and phrases and syntactic structures able to recall and describe ideal – and less than ideal – conditions (27–8)?

The potential for linguistic determinism relates to the second aspect of the Sapir–Whorf hypothesis, *cultural relativity*. It can do so in destructive ways. Certainly it is a root cause of Lok and the people's tragic end. For when Ha is first missing and thought to have gone voluntarily with 'the other man', Lok is positive that he and the strange newcomers will

'have changed words or shared a picture. Ha will tell us and I will go
after him.' He looked round at them. 'People understand each other.'

(71–2)

But Lok's confidence is of course sadly and pathetically misplaced. In
our own experience too, communication between people speaking
different languages is fraught with difficulty.

Part of the reason, according to Whorf, is that people are not 'led by
the same physical evidence to the same picture of the universe, unless
their linguistic backgrounds are similar, or can in some way be
calibrated' (Carroll and Wiley 1956: 214). He does not confine his
evidence to labels like nouns, but refers to syntax, arguing that the
grammar of a particular language not only helps its users to see the
world in a certain way but also limits perception. He appears to claim,
for example, that the space, time and matter of Newtonian physics could
not have been conceptualized in a language very different from English.

However, his point is frequently illustrated with reference to the
Eskimos' language for snow. Eskimos have many different words for
what they see as different kinds of snow. English has one (perhaps two,
if we include *slush*). Does this mean not simply that English speakers
may not (as discussed above in relation to the railway crisis of 1991) be
ready to deal with different kinds of snow but that, because we do not
have several assorted labels, we cannot even *recognize* all the varieties
– for example, falling snow, hard-packed snow, igloo-building snow –
that Eskimos find it necessary to note and label in their snow-bound
lives? Hardly. We can, as in this paragraph, construct phrases from the
vocabulary we do have to describe what we have had no difficulty in, on
reflection at least, recognizing. But this is a relatively trivial example
and it would seem that sometimes neither this sort of circumlocution
nor direct translation – substituting one word for another – helps to
bridge much more serious gaps between speakers of different languages. For example, in the Gulf crisis a professor of sociology at the
University of Jordan argued that offence caused to the west by Saddam
Hussein's use of the word *daif* was based on mistranslation (*Guardian*
11 November 1990: 27). English speakers took it to mean *guest* and
would certainly have preferred *hostage*, given the English words' very
different implications about free will. Yet, according to Sari Nasir, *daif*
means someone who is already in your home and therefore must be
given 'hospitality', whatever problem exists between host and *daif*.
Nevertheless, even if this had been made clear by interpreters, there
would surely have been cross-cultural dispute about the meaning of
hospitality.

It would therefore seem that whilst a language may not be an unchallengeable determiner, it can be a kind of 'irritant', pushing us, encouraging us towards certain ways of seeing and thinking. Consequently, Lok and his fellows would have been better equipped to comprehend, to give shape to and thus to cope with their experience, if (a) their language had been richer and (b) it had had more in common with that of the newcomers.

Nevertheless, failing these conditions, the original people could still have dealt more effectively with their lives, and with its fresh, unfamiliar experiences, if they had been adept in creating new language from their own existing foundations. We too may be hampered, to an extent, by linguistic determinism and cultural relativity but, as already suggested, we are potentially – though we may not always use our skill – much more creative than Lok and his fellows. This is true particularly in one respect. That is, we control *simile* and *metaphor* to powerful effect.

SIMILE AND METAPHOR

Neither simile nor metaphor are merely ornamental devices. They are uses of language which help to identify similarities between the old and the new, the familiar and the unfamiliar and, building on this recognition, they can make the unknown knowable.

Moreover, simile and metaphor are not restricted to the craft of the literary artist. In a sense, we are all artists, every day, for we employ these creative skills constantly to aid comprehension and communication.

Similes, of course, openly acknowledge a relationship perceived between two entities, experiences or concepts. They use the word *like*, or something of the sort: *This garden is **like** a jungle* or *Taking my exams I felt **as if** I were climbing a mountain*. The garden in question is presumably densely overgrown. Taking the exams must have felt a great challenge and effort like, the speaker assumes, tackling Everest.

By drawing deliberate attention to some aspect of perception in this way, similes may help their users gain control of situations and feelings. Call a garden a jungle and it is evident that vigorous action is needed to sort it out! Describing exam strain by comparing it to mountaineering may be a comfort, an encouragement, reminding the examinee that tests need not be a useless torture but can be a means to an end, to reaching a goal like the summit of a mountain.

Lok had been noticing comparisons all his life. For a long time he had thought that tree fungi had a lot in common with ears (194). But he had not drawn attention to similarities as a self-conscious and explanatory use of language. When he discovered he could do so it was a revelation. Suddenly he found himself

> in a convulsion of the understanding . . . using likeness as a tool as surely as ever he had used a stone to hack at sticks or meat. Likeness could grasp the white-faced hunters with a hand, could put them into the world where they were thinkable and not a random and unrelated irruption.
>
> (194)

Now they have been made 'thinkable' in this way, Lok understands the danger, and the aggression, and the power of the newcomers. For now he can see they are

> like a famished wolf in the hollow of a tree . . . like the river and the fall, they are a people of the fall; nothing stands against them.
>
> (194–5)

Even so, they have a strange and terrifying fascination. Fa believes the new people are 'like a fire in the forest' (197), and both Lok and Fa know that, once before, fire 'flew away and ate up the trees' (198). And yet these strangers are magnetic: 'Terrible they might be as the fire or the river but they drew like honey' (198). But which honey – the nourishing 'honey trickling from a crevice in a rock' or the treacherous 'honey in the round stones, the new honey that smells of dead things and fire' (195)?

Lok has discovered the power of likeness – yet he has come to it too late. This ability to understand, facilitated through linguistic comparison between the known and the unknown, is realized only after the new ones have begun to assume their ascendancy.

Besides, the newcomers have a greater complexity of imagination and of language: they go beyond simile to make metaphors. Lok did have the rudiments of this process. In metaphor, of course, two ideas are not (as they are in similes) openly linked by some such word as *like*. Instead, the one in some sense *becomes* the other: fungi on the trees were not simply 'like' ears for Lok – they *were* ears (194). They were ears, that is, in certain respects but not, as Lok is perfectly aware, in others: 'the word was the same but acquired a distinction by circumstances that could never apply to the sensitive things on the side of his head' (194). The point is that, through metaphor, we mentally borrow only certain aspects of an idea, an object or whatever, in order to highlight certain features of something else. Call a human being an 'angel', for instance, and presumably we indicate only qualities like goodness and beauty, and have forgotten the wings and halo that accompany these in the genuine article.

Still, though Lok uses metaphor he does so rarely and without the revealing, explanatory subtlety of Tuami and his fellows. Tuami begins with a simile – 'I am *like* a pool' – and extends to metaphor when he reflects

> some tide *has* filled me, the waters *are* obscured and strange things *are* creeping out of the cracks and crannies in my mind.
>
> (227; italics mine)

But Tuami is able to do more through the comparison of metaphor than describe his present state of mind. Recognizing in Vivani and the infant some resemblance to the ivory haft of his knife, he uses the parallel to clarify and confirm to himself an insight – an insight which could have profound implications for his life, both now and in the future.

He has been afraid, confused, angry. A metaphor explains: 'The sand was swirling in Tuami's brain' (229). He had been grinding the blade of his dagger, grinding it to a killing sharpness and contemplating murdering Marlan with the 'ivory-point'. But now he is struck by the futility of murder in present circumstances, and so, at the same time, the ivory haft which he must grip to drive home a killing blow, feels a 'shapeless lump', without significance.

> There was no power in his hands and no picture in his head. Neither the blade nor the haft was important in these waters. For a moment he was tempted to throw the thing overboard.
>
> (232)

But the knife, the haft though not its blade, will soon become important – *perceptually* powerful. For the feel of its handle's rough but graspable shape will become an inspiration, a clue to surviving the present moment and a possible way into the future. Because, as Tuami considers further, he remoulds and clarifies his ideas through metaphor and now, in a way that is related to the knife, an image of Vivani and the child becomes a 'password' (233).

For, struggling and wriggling, the 'little one' appears from within Vivani's furs, 'his little rump pushing against the nape of her neck'. The woman – loving, fearful, defiant – rubs 'her cheek sideways against the curly hair' (233). This ludicrous spectacle convulses the people with laughter, and Tuami lets the ivory fall from his hands. Its murderous blade is no longer important as fear recedes, the swirling sands in his head sinking back to the bottom of the pool, his mind clearing as he begins to perceive order, control and purpose. For the rump and the head now seem to him to fit together. They make of the confusing and the frightening a coherent shape, a shape of love, need and laughter – a shape that (equally rough but equally precious) can be managed and held comfortably in the mind just as the ivory haft can be physically contained in the hand.

> They were waiting in the rough ivory of the knife-haft that was so much more important than the blade. They were an answer, the frightened, angry love of the woman and the ridiculous, intimidating rump that was wagging at her head, they were a password. His hand felt for the ivory in the bilges and he could feel in his fingers how Vivani and her devil fitted it.

(233)

As Tuami thinks in this way, in terms of an *answer* and a *password*, he is dealing in metaphors, borrowing some of the usual implications of these words.

Now, when he looks ahead to the far side of the lake, he cannot see if the line of darkness there has an ending. Yet, whatever he will find when he has crossed the water, he has potential to survive, for in his powers of understanding is a constructive imagination, developed by his language. On this occasion it has given him hope and peace and so, holding firmly to the knife's ivory haft, Tuami begins to relax into sleep.

Metaphor is part of our own survival kit, but it is not without difficulties. For, as already suggested, metaphors are not (in a number of ways, discussed in chapter 4, which relates Susan Sontag's essay *AIDS and its Metaphors* (1990) to Lakoff and Johnson's *Metaphors we Live by* (1980)), perfect matches with reality.

It is so with Tuami's password metaphor. In Golding's usage it suggests the idea of a key (another metaphor, daily used) to entry. However, entry by password is supposed, by definition, to be certain, designed to give automatic admission. Yet Vivani and the child's mix of feelings (love, anger, humour) – though available to Tuami and, as they combine and fit together in some appealing sense, a possible way forward, an entry to the future – are not, being human and unpredictable, unlike passwords, automatically within his control and certain to be effective. We have seen that Lok realized the limitations of *ear* as a suitable metaphor for a piece of fungus, but this was a very simple and obvious case of imperfect fit. The use of *password* for Vivani and the child is clearly much more complex and subtle. Yet if Tuami does not take account of the anomalies in this metaphor then his understanding will be limited, perhaps dangerously self-deceiving. As for the knife (a visible and tangible, as well as linguistic, metaphor) its haft is precious and, despite its roughness, may be comfortably grasped, but a destructive blade is still waiting, half-formed on this uneven hilt, and should not be forgotten.

However, the making of metaphor is only one linguistic means to survival, a means not fully possessed by Lok though practised by Tuami and by ourselves. There is another language skill that we employ with great sophistication but which, again, Lok has only in a rudimentary fashion: that is, the ability to organize language into connected structures, including the elements of narrative. Narrative is discussed immediately below and in more detail in chapter 5.

NARRATIVE STRUCTURING

Language appears to help the newcomers, and certainly ourselves, to separate ideas and then put them into meaningful relationships and sequences. Some of these combine to form the potentially reasoning, explanatory device of a story.

Lok, however, has difficulty with the creative art of sorting and ordering. For example, having seen the inheritors for the first time he is bewildered: 'There were so many things to be said': if only he knew 'what it was that joined a picture to a picture so that the last of many came out of the first' (96).

At the very least, giving parts of his pictures word labels would have separated them into component bits – though the limitations of Lok's lexicon would, if the Whorfian hypothesis is correct to some degree, restrict his perception of its elements.

Then, putting the words into syntactic clauses would have identified 'actors' and the 'acted upon' – a vital further step which will be returned to below in a discussion of *transitivity*.

Next, arranging the clauses one after the other would have suggested some sort of sequencing. This sequencing might indicate order of importance: there was this, that and the other in a relative hierarchy of significance. It could also, or instead, imply chronology: this happened first, then that and finally the other.

Of course it is possible to speak of matters out of order, but lexical and syntactic manipulation can reassert hierarchical or temporal logic. For example, with regard to time, the sentence *Fa grinned after Lok had told her he would bring home a deer*, speaks of the second action first, but the adverb *after* and the verb phrase *had told* counteract any impression that Fa's grin actually occurred before Lok's boast.

Putting things in chronological order is at the crux of *story-telling*. Narration is an aspect of language behaviour practised by people in widely diverse cultures (Mandler 1984: 50–3) and sophisticated tale-telling can be a potent heuristic, explanatory device, for it can be used, as Sarbin has suggested, and as discussed below, 'as a guide to living and as a vehicle for understanding the conduct of others' (Sarbin 1986: x).

Sometimes Lok did manage this kind of linguistic organization. Although that first meeting with the newcomers was beyond his linguistic capacities and remained bewildering, he loved to recount the happenings surrounding his discovery of the little Oa. In telling of his picture – which makes the people laugh because it was 'almost the only one he had' (33) – Lok appears virtually transported back to the time of the happening itself, for he retells the events in the present tense.

'– I am standing among the trees. I feel. . . . What do I feel? A bulb? A stick? A bone?. . . . It is the little Oa! . . . And now where Liku is there is the little Oa.'

(33)

However, on the whole, story-telling seems to be in its infancy with the people, for it generally lacks what Labov has termed *evaluation* (Labov and Waletsky 1967: Labov 1972: Labov and Fanshel 1977) and it is principally this which gives narration its potential to 'guide' and to explain living.

Lok's tale of the little Oa's discovery does, it is true, have some of the other components Labov isolates in narratives. It has, for instance, an *abstract* (which Labov finds optional), a quick summary given before the story proper: 'I have a picture – . . . of finding the little Oa'.

Then, in Lok's story as in other narratives, comes the essential core of any tale, the *complication*, made up of clauses which 'recapitulate experience in the same order as the original events' (Helms 1967: 20–21). If this chronology is altered then nonsense may result: Lok could hardly have felt the bone and *then* stood amongst the trees. Alternatively a totally different story may be constructed by altering the sequencing. For instance – to leave Lok's narrative on one side for a moment – if in the nursery rhyme of Jack and Jill the children had been able to fetch water *before* climbing the hill, hampered with cumbersome buckets, the whole sorry affair might have been prevented.

Then, stories may or may not have a *result*: in nursery rhyme Jack's case, having gone up the hill and tumbled down it, he ended up in bed, his head wrapped in vinegar and brown paper.

Finally, and crucially, there may or may not be an *evaluation* of the story. 'Jack and Jill went up the hill – they fetched some water – Jack fell down' is, given its chronologically related clauses, a story in the simplest sense but, lacking some assessment of these events, hearers are likely to wonder 'So what? Why was the story told? What is its point?' If it is present at all, evaluation may come right at the end of the tale in the form of a clear judgement: 'Children like Jack and Jill should never be asked to carry heavy pails up and down hills'. Alternatively, evaluation can be woven into the fabric of the story: 'Jack and Jill, carrying *ridiculously* heavy pails, trudged *laboriously* up the hill and, *not surprisingly*, overbalanced down again'. These interwoven assessments suggest a cautionary tale, warning parents against the folly of overburdening and consequently overturning their children. Still, whether something of the sort was meant by the nursery rhyme we cannot know because its creator left no evaluation of the unfortunate happening!

No matter: children reciting the rhyme seem unperturbed. But then, very young children do not themselves evaluate the tales they tell. At first they produce a kind of haphazard sequencing, what Rothery and Martin (1980) have termed a 'recount', jumping back and forth across events, not making clear which might have happened first or last: 'Jack's head had brown paper on it. He went up the hill. He fell down. He wanted a pail. He went with Jill'. This process gives way to a rational-seeming chronological sequencing which, as Peterson and McCabe point out (1983), ends around the age of five at some sort of high point – in Jack's case, presumably, the brown-paper treatment.

To return now to Lok's tale of Oa, its conclusion – 'And now where Liku is there is the little Oa' (33) – seems to fall somewhere between simple result and evaluation, for the consequence that Liku now possesses the significantly shaped root alludes obliquely to the success and purpose of Lok's rooting around in the earth.

But more complex evaluation seems beyond Lok. In order for assessments to be expressed regularly and potently on the Labovian model, Lok and the people would need to be more adept with the facility of displacement, to have a developed concept of time, a more effective long-term memory and probably greater intelligence. As it is, without the partly linguistic power of narration, Lok and the people are as children, simply recounting, their understanding of experience limited. True, Mal is sometimes successful in reasoning through story-telling. When the log has disappeared he has a picture. He places his hand 'flat on his head as if confining the images that flickered there' and tells the waiting people,

> 'Mal is not old but clinging to his mother's back. There is more water not only here but along the trail where we came. A man is wise. He makes the men take a tree that has fallen and–'.

(15)

His memory is so clear that, like Lok narrating the Oa happening, Mal is telling the story in the present tense. But he does not complete it. He breaks off without giving either its result or any evaluation of the tale's significance. Instead he turns to the people, 'imploring them to share' (16) the picture and, most importantly, to grasp its point. But they are unable to make a deduction from the events he has described. Ha says, 'I do not see this picture' and Mal has to help him, extracting from his picture the essential point of his remembering, evaluating it to discover the strategy that can guide the people over the water. He sighs and says, 'Find a tree that has fallen' (16).

This ability to mull over experience and in the process to make sense of it, evaluating it for present and future reference, is essential for survival, learning by experience. Indeed, what happens to us may not even be truly 'experienced' until we give it thought and the judging shape of language. Crites, making a distinction between 'sense' and 'experience', argues:

> many things are experienced retroactively. The close air, my laboured breath, my co-worker's agitation had to be sensed at the time [of their happening] or they could not have dawned on me later, and of course it is common to use the word 'experience' for all such sensations. . . .
> I prefer to say that most of the things that are sensed are never experienced, and that only those that are attended to are.
>
> (Sarbin 1986: 160)

Lok's senses are acute, much more so in some ways than ours. After Ha's disappearance there 'built up in Lok's head a picture of the man [the other], not by reasoned deduction but because in every place the scent told him – do this! As the smell of cat would evoke in him a cat-stealth of avoidance and a cat-snarl' (77). But this response is involuntary. Unlike ourselves, Lok has not formed the habit of deliberately contemplating sensations. Yet if Lok and the people do not, voluntarily and consciously, consider an event they may not truly experience it: their sensations remain uncontrolled. Consequently, particularly in respect of narratives, they cannot learn from experience. As they cannot, through language, possess their past in order to deal with the present, their ability to evolve and survive is severely limited.

Once, it is true, Lok thought he had taken on Mal's superior perceptual power and it 'seemed to him that his head was new, as though a sheaf of pictures lay there to be sorted out when he would' (191). But his confidence was short-lived and soon pictures 'went from his head again and he became nothing but a vast well of feeling that could not be examined or denied' (193).

Nor, unlike ourselves, can Lok and the people adapt narrative techniques and use them to help plan for the future. In the people, the ability to look forward is only rudimentary – though the woman, Fa, does have some predictive capability.

LANGUAGING A FUTURE

Today some feminists are suspicious of logical thinking. They may reject its power and clarity as oppressive, cold – and therefore, in their view, 'male'. They value instead the emphasis of emotion, indicated perhaps through marked intonational and rhythmic emphasis. For them this kind of utterance is 'feminine'. (See chapter 7 for a development of these points.)

To some extent Lok and the people share this view: they are more in awe of the spiritual, creative power of Oa, which they sense in all women, than they are of the rudimentary power of thoughtful 'picturing', which they see as a male skill: 'As long as there was a woman there was life. But what use was a man save for smelling things out and having pictures?', Lok wondered (85).

But they also know the pictures are vital and in truth Fa, the woman, is rather better than Lok at managing her pictured thoughts. She sarcastically compares his ability with a baby's: 'You have fewer pictures than the new one' (134).

Crucially, Fa can make some constructive use of displacement to tell a story, not only of the past, but also for the future. In this way she can image a chronology of likely events and hypothesize their causal links and results: she declares with confidence, 'We will take Tanakil. *Then* they will give back the new one' (213; italics mine). Lok's skill in this respect is confined to unfounded optimism – 'When the new people bring Liku back I shall be glad' (133) – and to sheer fantasy, like his boasting prediction of bringing a surfeit of food, the quarters of a cow beneath one arm, deer beneath another (37–8). He cannot easily follow Fa in her reasoning and future planning. Her pictured plan of them 'crossing to the island on the log' is at first incomprehensible to him and even after she has patiently re-explained he soon forgets her reasoning (120–1).

Given Fa's assessing, planning capability, facilitated by language skills that reason with the past and look forward to the future, she might have coped in the inheritors' world – just. But even Fa's skill is imperfect. When she had a picture of the people emptying shells she was 'frustrated by the vivid detail . . ., not knowing how to extract from it the significance she felt was there' (62).

The inheritors, on the other hand, have far more pictures (126), and far more capacity to analyse them, using a rich lexicon, the skill of metaphoring and the telling structure of narration. Their language, and the use they make of it, will help them to survive and evolve into the future.

When, in Golding's chapter 12 (223–5), we enter the minds of the newcomers, we witness the full extent of their mental and linguistic sophistication. We discover that Tuami can, in addition to the metaphoring we have already discussed, *wonder* about and *judge* data (223). Only weariness prevents him from using his ability to *balance* information in order to make *calculations* and reach *conclusions* (224). Moreover, he can look back and consider what might have happened in the story of their lives *if* things had been different: 'for with [the great square sail] and the breeze through the gap he need not have endured these hours of strain' (223). And he can look forward, predicting possible stories, foretelling their events, results, significances – and thus being prepared for the future in a way quite beyond Lok: '*If* the breeze changed or faltered those lines *would*' do such and such (223–4); '*Perhaps* if they squared off the boat' such and such would happen (225). All in all, Tuami and the tribe can *think* of the past, *assess* the present, *intend* for the future (223, 225, 226).

There is also another respect in which the people and the inheritors differ radically: that is, in their choices from language's *transitivity system*, choices which tend to empower the newcomers for the future whilst disenabling Lok and his fellows. It is not that Lok does not have or cannot use transitivity – unlike his lack of vocabulary and his limited skill in metaphoring and in evaluative narration – but rather that he uses it in a way which reflects a world quite different from the one understood by the inheritors.

THE SYNTAX OF POWER

M.A.K. Halliday drew attention to a difference between Lok and Tuami in terms of transitivity in his *Explorations in the Functions of Language* (1973). He argued that the 'theme of the entire novel, in a sense, is transitivity: man's interpretation of his experience of the world, his understanding of its processes and of his own participation in them' (134). What follows here does not precisely match Halliday's much more detailed argument, but it borrows from his thesis and arrives at very similar conclusions.

In English, verbs are transitive or intransitive, or have the potential to be either. Transitive verbs can take an object (*he killed* **him**): intransitives do not (*he died*). Some verbs can do either, like *grow*: a gardener may grow a plant, or the plant may grow. Transitives can therefore stress the power of what might be termed an 'agent' or 'actor' over another being or entity: intransitives do not – they keep themselves to themselves. But there is an 'affected' participant in both transitive and intransitive structures. In intransitives the initiator of action of some kind (including mental as well as physical activity) and the affected are combined in one participant: (*he died*; *she thought quickly*).

Lok and the people do use transitives – and transitives in which they themselves are agents. They speak of Mal cutting a stone (31), Lok beating a rock (24). And sometimes they acknowledge, through the transitivity system, their recognition that people can act upon each other, as well as upon inert objects: they talk of feeding the new one (131) and of placing Mal in the warm earth (87). (But see Short 1992 for an alternative explanation.)

However, sometimes the people identify what we, with modern knowledge, would say were the wrong agents. Golding, as narrator, is evidently using the people's language choices when he writes that Lok's feet 'saw' and 'threw him round' the beech roots (11). Moreover, Lok seems to think that his ears have a separate life, can themselves be actors and can 'speak' to him (43). It would therefore appear that the people do not always recognize the control they have over their own bodies and minds. Moreover, they sometimes invest the natural world with what, to us, is human behaviour and feeling: for them the fire 'wakes' (30), the water 'sleeps' (12). These are apparently not examples of our modern-day, self-conscious personification but express a genuine belief that the fire and the water are 'affected participants'.

In sum, Lok and the people are not linguistically immature in respect of the transitivity system, and they do have an understanding of causality, of one entity producing an effect upon another. But this understanding is naive – and so limits their ability to think about and to preserve themselves from the assertive power of the inheritors.

It is not of course surprising – and certainly not to their moral discredit – that the people's comprehension is naive in this respect. The people have never before encountered behaviour like the tribe's and Lok can hardly select syntax that identifies aggressive agency when this is something that, in Crites' terminology (referred to above, p. 26), he has never 'sensed'. Nor can he bridge gaps in his understanding with metaphor if he has no known point of contact with which to compare the fresh and the puzzling. He certainly cannot imagine narratives that are totally unfamiliar, outside his ken. And so much is outside his ken because the 'sensations' available for Lok and the people to experience, with the help of language, have been quite different from those familiar to the newcomers.

For one thing Lok, Ha, Fa, Nil and the others are, in their sharing, loving, protective behaviour towards each other, more a group than they are separate individuals. Their feeling for community can be seen in their deep, shared silences. At such times they may have what Golding describes as a 'passion of pity for each other' (132). And they have a kind of group telepathy, a joint, silent picturing of the sort they experience when, together, they realize that Mal knows he will soon die (38–9). By contrast, the inheritors vere towards an assertive individualism. Their experience includes an aggressive, jealous, competitive, achieving – separate – sense of self.

In consequence Tuami's use of transitivity shows his recognition of individual power. He is well aware that *he* shoots the arrow, hoists the sails, paddles the boat (albeit in competition with natural forces that threaten to capsize it). But, as Halliday points out, when the more innocent Lok peers through the bushes at the newcomers, to his inexperienced eye 'the stick began to grow shorter at both ends. Then it shot out to full length again' (106). Evidently, whilst Tuami, and we, recognize the stick as a bow that is inert and ineffective without human agency, Lok has no idea that a man could – must – be responsible for this bow causing a 'lump of bone' to cross the river. Therefore there will be no transitive verb like *shoot* in Lok's lexicon, no structures to pinpoint and clarify the action ('the stick and the bone can shoot Lok') for him. The gentle Lok cannot label the sticks and bone and feathers he sees as he peers through the bushes as a 'bow' and an 'arrow', much less as a 'weapon', for he has no sense of the menace they carry, at least when in human control. And because he has never before encountered anything else with similar properties to a flying, killing twig and bone, he cannot borrow from the known to create an appropriate metaphor that will help him comprehend the destructive unknown.

And yet, ironically, though Lok does not recognize the inheritors' destructive strength, Tuami (as Halliday points out (131)) perceives this kind of power in the people. In the last sixteen pages of the novel Lok and the others are, to the inheritors, 'devils', who have driven the new tribe away from the mountains. Yet this vision is surely in the minds and language of the inheritors: the people's so-called power is a perception depending more upon Tuami's 'advanced' concepts of aggressive humanity than their actual strength and behaviour.

SURVIVAL BY LANGUAGE

We too are more competitive, more individual selves than parts of a co-operative group like Lok's. But at least the inheritors, and we, generally maintain some sort of linguistic communication and community – however complicated, difficult, sometimes creative and often destructive these are. We have, we could say by contrast with Lok at the end of his story, the powerful energy of humanness.

For Lok becomes 'it'. When every one of the people but he is dead, when he has lost his part in the people's group, when he has no one of his own kind to belong to, and no one to communicate with, then, inevitably, Lok loses language, loses this significant mark of humanness and reverts to the animal, to a red creature, smallish and bowed. Lok is no longer 'he' but 'it' – and 'it' no longer sees pictures, speaks them, tries to think them through. The only shred of humanness left to it is the ability to cry, the tears swimming down the silvered curls of its beard when the poor, pathetic, crouching animal discovers the bones of Liku and knows it is alone.

Without communion and communication it can only crawl, noiseless, towards the ashes of the fire, lie on its side, pulling its legs up, knees against its chest, its hands folded beneath its cheek and, becoming quite still, grow into the earth and wait for death.

But the inheritors survive. For they are not only temperamentally more self-assertive. Additionally, and equally importantly, they have, like Lok, all the design features of language but, unlike him, they put these to more effective use, evolving lexicon, metaphor and also a story line, adjusting perceptions of its 'agents' as their encounters and understanding develop.

The process continues. We ourselves, seeing from a different angle, understand things differently from Tuami and so, for instance, would be unlikely to call Lok and the people 'devils'. And, to turn from fiction to fact, whilst, for example, Francis Bacon (1561–1626) certainly had in his lexicon, as Kress and Hodge point out (1979: 41–53), a multitude of both transitive and intransitive verbs, his knowledge led him to use some of them differently than we, with our increased understanding, do today. For Bacon wrote that 'many substances in nature which are solid do putrify and corrupt into worms': *they* corrupt. We, however, do not use 'corrupt' intransitively: we say an agent corrupts something else. But then, since Pasteur, it has become clear to us that putrifaction and corruption are caused by something, by bacteria.

No doubt, if we are to continue to survive, our language will continue to change. It will alter as we think it – and our inheritance – through.

SUGGESTIONS FOR FURTHER WORK

1 Take an incident from *The Inheritors*, involving the people, and reword it as if it were being experienced today, by ourselves. That is, where appropriate, change vocabulary and syntax (particularly with regard to agency and transitivity), introducing metaphor and narrative structuring if necessary.

Explain why you have felt it right, as a twentieth-century person, to make each alteration. In other words, what do the changes imply about modern perceptions and behaviour, and about the power of the language we use?

The first lines of the novel ('Lok was running . . . the log was gone') would be suitable for this exercise, particularly with regard to transitivity.

2 Bearing in mind Lok and Tuami's different perceptions of their world, consider Deirdre Burton's argument (in Carter 1982a: 200) that 'once it is clear to people that there are alternative ways of expressing "reality", then people can make decisions about how to express "reality": both for others and themselves. By this means, we can both deconstruct and *reconstruct* our realities to an enabling degree'. Burton illustrates her argument through discussion of an extract from Sylvia Plath's novel *The Bell Jar*. A similar point of view is expressed in chapter 5 of *Literature about Language*.

3 Are there aspects of your life which you feel your language is inadequate to express? (For example, some women believe the English language is incomplete with regard to female experience.) If so, could you consciously create new words or new metaphors to help you consider them? Does any new language you develop for this purpose help you to extend your understanding – and thus, in a sense, your survival?

2   Linguistic creativity and limitation
'my sweet old etcetera' by e. e. cummings

The poem 'my sweet old etcetera' is discussed in relation to aspects of linguistic creativity with particular regard to structure dependency, morphology and 'chain and choice'. Uses of language (as well as the poem itself) are considered: these include feminist choices, Rastafarian English and 'anti-languages'.

my sweet old etcetera
aunt lucy during the recent

war could and what
is more did tell you just
what everybody was fighting

for,
my sister

isabel created hundreds
(and
hundreds) of socks not to
mention shirts fleaproof earwarmers

etcetera wristers etcetera, my
mother hoped that

i would die etcetera
bravely of course my father used
to become hoarse talking about how it was
a privilege and if only he
could meanwhile my

self etcetera lay quietly
in the deep mud et

cetera
(dreaming,
et
   cetera, of
Your smile
eyes knees and of your Etcetera)
   (Firmage 1981: 275, first published 1926 in *is 5*.)

cummings' poem is about war: it is also about the human capacity for linguistic creativity – and about the limitations, including avoidance and self-deception, imposed upon that powerful ability.

Choosing the word *etcetera*, cummings describes family reactions to a relation's involvement in war (specifically, no doubt, the 1914–18 war, as cummings himself was at the front in 1917 with the American Ambulance Corps). Since *etcetera* means something like 'and the rest, and so on' or, as a plural noun, 'sundries, minor additions', it is safe to assume irony in its reference to grave and terrible circumstances. It is the precise and varying implications of this irony that make the poem disturbing (but also, in a way, humorous) and it is the manner of the word's selection which is so revealing about human language, about the powerful creativity it gives us and about the limits imposed upon that creativity.

For there are paradoxes in the concept of language creativity. We 'choose' language: but it also chooses us. We are, to use linguistic terminology, 'structure-dependent' and 'rule-governed'; yet that dependence and government is also our freedom.

The American linguist, Noam Chomsky, has emphasized (1957, 1959, 1965) this rule-based nature of language and argued that we are born predisposed to recognize such rules. Some of his ideas have been challenged in recent years, and his own thinking has developed significantly, but a basic Chomskyan principle, that children acquire language not through simple imitation (merely repeating the utterances they hear around them) but in part through identifying and then working from the rules of the language of their particular environment, seems indisputable. We have all heard small children making mistakes like *She **goed** to the farm. She **seed** sheeps there.* These errors are no cause for alarm. On the contrary, such children appear to have realized that, in English, adding the suffix 'morpheme' (see below) *ed* to verbs frequently creates a past tense, and adding the morpheme *s* frequently – as a rule, that is – turns singular nouns into plurals. These rules are not consciously acknowledged of course (and at this age the speaker certainly does not possess the metalanguage used here to describe the process) but, without formal instruction, s/he has identified a rule and, until exceptions are noted, is simply overextending it for the time being. (See Aitchison 1989 for a most readable and comprehensive discussion of language and its acquisition and the relative linguistic capacity, referred to below, of animals.)

These rules – which are not matters of taste and good manners but are a creative necessity – are related to *structure*. Working with structure seems to be a defining feature of our humanness (see chapter 1). Attempts to teach human language to animals, particularly chimpanzees, have been successful only up to a point – the point of structure-dependence.

Word order, for example, is an important – creative – aspect of structuring, especially in English. A word gains some of its meaning from its place in a sentence: change its place and the same word is given the power to mean differently. *The car hit the bus* does not mean the same thing as *The bus hit the car*. Even young children seem to use structure in this way. English children apparently put the subject of a sentence before the action, the object or location after the action: *teddy wash, wash teddy, go school*. However, whilst a chimpanzee called Washoe, in an American research project in the 1960s, acquired a reasonable vocabulary (of sign language) and correctly attributed different words to different situations, she did not seem to recognize the significance and creative potential of word order. When asking to be taken to the raspberry patch for her favoured fruit, she was as likely to sign 'Sweet go' as 'Go sweet', both apparently meaning 'Take me to the raspberry bushes'. More recent experiments with other chimps have had similar results and do not seem to disprove Chomsky's belief that apes 'apparently lack the capacity to develop even the rudiments of the computational structure of human language' (1980: 57).

On the other hand, given a group of ordered words, some animals have appeared to understand the simpler but infinitely creative structural manoeuvre of 'slot filling'. That is, sentences may be imagined as having slots into which any one of a number of suitable words could be inserted. We could choose, for instance, to replace *icy* in the following sentence by something like *muddy* or *wet* or *dangerous*. And we could replace *slipped* by *fell* or *stumbled*.

(1) When I got off the bus, I slipped on that icy pavement by the post office.

There are, as it were, two axes, horizontal and vertical. We arrange the slots of sentences on a horizontal 'chain', verbs, nouns, adjectives, adverbs and so on having rightful places in the line-up or *syntagm*. We know the syntactic rules of these arrangements and so recognize – though Washoe would probably not have done – that, in sentence (1), the noun *path* cannot be switched with the verb *slipped*. But our choice is not limited to 'syntagmatic' syntactic patterns. There is also a vertical axis of choice, the 'pile' or *paradigm* of suitable words from which we can select for each slot, nouns for noun slots, verbs for verb slots and so on.

the icy pavement
muddy
wet
dangerous

Of course, these choices will usually be suitable in the semantic as well as the syntactic sense. We are not very likely, in this context, to substitute something like *sleepy* or *egocentric* here (though poetry might permit otherwise).

Lana, a chimpanzee trained in the 1970s, did become adept at simple slot filling. She communicated by pressing keys marked with symbols representing words. Given a sentence like *Tim give Lana milk*, she could replace *milk* with *juice* or *coke*. However, it is unlikely that Lana or any other chimpanzee has understood – as human language users certainly do – that some groups of words form units. These groups can be replaced, with more words or fewer, then left where they are or else moved. We appreciate that, in sentence (1), *on that icy pavement by the post office* or just *by the post office* could be regarded as units and replaced by something like *there*. And *When I got off the bus* could be replaced by *then*. We also know that all these groups of words, or their single substitutes, could be pulled out of their original slots and moved to other suitable ones. For instance, *I slipped there, then*.

So, in sum, whilst such structural manoeuvres may not be known to animals, the finite rules of a particular language give to its human users the potential for infinite creativity. We can produce and understand sentences we have never heard before; we are not parrots. Lewis Carroll's poem, 'Jabberwocky', including structures like ''Twas brillig, and the slithy toves/Did gyre and gimble in the wabe', would be a bizarre and extreme example of this ability, for though its vocabulary includes words that, before the poem's conception at least, could not be found in a dictionary, we can still make some sort of sense from the lines because their words are structured according to English syntactic and morphological rules. We know, for instance, that 'slithy' is probably an adjective and 'toves' is a noun because we are familiar with nouns following *the*, often with an intervening adjective that sometimes ends in the morpheme *y*, and because we know (without conscious deliberation) that nouns are frequently pluralized by adding *s*.

Moreover, we are not forced by external circumstances to create particular groups of words. Chomsky (1959) demolished the psychologist B.F. Skinner's view (1957) that we produce predictable language in response to particular stimuli – like hungry caged rats learn to press the right bar in order to be rewarded with food. Stimuli cannot be said to control our linguistic reactions in such a rigid and automatic way since these are so variable. A sudden rain shower might be followed by *I'm soaked*. But any number of utterances, some of them without immediately obvious links to the rain, could be inspired just as easily: *I forgot my umbrella*, *Let's get a taxi*, *Corfu was never like this*.

So why, given this infinite creativity and resourcefulness, do we ever resort to choosing empty phrases, clichés and platitudes? Why do we opt for bland, unconsidered fillers of which *etcetera* is an example and symbol?

The obvious answer, using Chomskyan terminology, is that whilst we all have linguistic *competence* – knowledge, more or less unconsciously stored, about language and its rule-generated potential – when we put that knowledge into *performance* there are limits, some of them self-imposed, some of them not, upon the choices that we make from our available resources. The speaker may be limited for a number of reasons – habitual, perceptual, emotional, intellectual, psychological, cultural, social. Time, memory and simple vocabulary gaps are other possible constraints.

In the poem, the word *etcetera*, though literally meaning 'and the rest' or 'minor additions' and therefore being essentially a noun phrase, is chosen to fill a variety of different syntactic slots – noun, adjective, verb and so on – along the syntagm. It is saying something like 'and the rest of those semantically possible nouns (adjectives or verbs and so on) in the paradigm'. Either the speaker cannot think of a more specific and relevant noun, verb, adjective or whatever, or for some reason prefers not to do so.

On the other hand, it would appear that sometimes, in the poem, *etcetera* has been chosen, not through lack of available language or through deliberate evasiveness, but in order to invite the hearer (guided by surrounding words and structures) to actively consider words for which it could stand, words of which the speaker is perfectly well aware but which for one reason or another – perhaps tact, perhaps private complicity with the listener – s/he has chosen not to select from the relevant syntactic and semantic paradigm but instead has decided to suppress.

These substituted, or repressed, words are likely to be clear to the reader, because we are guided by the narrating voice through the conventional procedure that hearers/readers appear to follow when responding to language. That is, language is not simply received passively on our mental screens but is actively processed. Because of the speed with which we are bombarded with words, this involves some preliminary assumptions, some common-sense guesswork, and some sifting and selecting.

The procedure is far more complex than there is space here to explain, and in any case there are still uncertainties surrounding it (again, Aitchison 1989: chapter 10 provides a detailed and very readable account). However, it is probably true to say that hearers/readers start by assuming each utterance consists of sentence-like bits, that (in English) include a noun phrase followed by a verb with the option of a further noun phrase. In the first instance, until any contrary evidence is perceived, this NP–V–NP sequence will be interpreted as actor–action–object. Then, we assume that people generally make sense. Therefore, selecting from the possibilities we know to be available, we anticipate words, or interpret them, in ways that fit semantically both surrounding language and our knowledge of the world.

This habitual procedure of anticipation and interpretation is not normally in the forefront of our minds, consciously done. But if, in relation to 'my sweet old etcetera', we now follow it deliberately, looking in turn at each example of *etcetera* and filling its place on the syntagm more precisely, the progress should be revealing both about the meaning of the poem and about human linguistic behaviour. We shall need to bear in mind, of course, that whilst words are *denotative*, having directly referential meanings which may be verified in a dictionary, they also have *connotations*, meanings arising from surrounding language structures, from other words with which they tend to collocate and, also, from the circumstances in which, in our experience, they are normally used. Since we do not all share precisely the same knowledge and experience, our anticipations and interpretations may vary.

'MY SWEET OLD ETCETERA'

In reading the poem we are drawn to experience the potential of linguistic creativity. We also witness its limitations. There is creativity, in which the reader is involved, in the first three and last four uses of the word *etcetera*. On these occasions *etcetera* is chosen by the poem's speaker and seems to point openly to more precise meanings that are, as it were, behind it in the paradigm. By contrast, this persona's parents appear to use the word because, for whatever reason, they do not want to confront its more precise alternatives. However, even in these circumstances, the reader, whilst witnessing limitation, is still drawn into the creative process of filling *etcetera*'s ambiguous slot.

Since *etcetera* is casually imprecise in its meaning ('and the rest') or downbeat ('sundries' or 'minor additions'), the poem has a superficial jokiness. But considering the word more carefully reveals a sharper edge. Take its very first use – 'my sweet old etcetera'. Speakers of English know from experience that words inserted between pronouns and nouns are generally modifiers and so are likely to assume that here *etcetera* is filling a third adjectival slot. If we choose something that *sweet* and *old* encourage us to expect, we could come up with *gentle* or (with a stress pattern to more or less maintain the poem's rhythm) *retiring*. But, as the poem gets underway, the reader learns that Lucy is likely to be many things apart from sweet and old, and these do not include gentle or retiring. On the contrary, Lucy is given to assertively lecturing on 'what everybody was fighting / for' – a subject about which she is likely to have little information and no experience. In fact, she is exploiting her own language creativity for all she is worth, making maximum use of *displacement* (see chapter 1), the human capacity to talk about matters far removed in time and space from the speaker and, in the absence of their corroboration, to create language of distortion, lies and fantasy as well as fact. Yet the poem's persona seems prevented – by delicacy or more probably sarcasm – from explicitly labelling a garrulous ignorance that is at odds with sweetness. No matter: in its blandness, *etcetera* invites the reader, guided by the poem's hint of her chattering arrogance, to describe the 'talkative', 'opinionated' Aunt Lucy for himself/herself.

Not everyone, however, is talking: Isabel is quietly sewing and knitting. And this time *etcetera* entices the reader to imagine a couple of slots filled not with adjectives but with yet more nouns, more objects to add to the socks and shirts and fleaproof earwarmers and wristers. The pile of comforters, *etcetera*'s expansive vagueness implies, is enormous and comprehensive: you name it, sister Isabel creates it.

But whilst Lucy is actively proclaiming, and Isabel is silently but energetically productive, the soldier's mother and father are using language – yet, in reality, saying little. Because, now, *etcetera* seems to be a substitute not for an abundance of ideas or images, known but unspecified by the speaker and left for the reader to consider at will (an abundance of personality defects in the case of Lucy and of garments in the case of Isabel), but for some kind of paucity, maybe of courage, thought or feeling, in the person who chooses to use it.

For why are the ordeals that *etcetera* might indicate, apart from dying, not named by the mother who hopes her son will die – and so on – bravely? Is it because she knows their terrors but prefers not to face them, mentally, with the son who must meet them physically? Perhaps, if so, this is out of consideration for the young man. Or perhaps, fearing for her son, this mother needs the word's protection for herself, the deliberate blindness which could allow her to imagine death as swift and merciful. On the other hand, are the horrors of war left unarticulated through ignorance, because this mother really does not know – has not been told, could not possibly imagine or does not want to consider even privately – what else, apart from death, her son might have to endure? Or, are the trials the word might be standing in for (particularly since *etcetera* is slotted in *after die*) merely of secondary importance to her, not really worth mentioning beside death? Even this last is just possible, given First World War propaganda that encouraged mothers to sacrifice their sons for a noble cause.

In any event, for whatever reason, the woman who chooses *etcetera* appears vague about its possible implications. But still, in its blandness, *etcetera* invites the reader to fill the void which the mother prefers to leave – and if we hesitate we could be reminded of our own inadequacies of knowledge or of courage.

As for the father, there is not even an *etcetera* to fill the gaps that our knowledge of English syntactic structure tells us exist in this parent's limited language. What, precisely, was the privilege he does not name? Just what was it that he wished to do? Does he mean he would, if only he could, go to war himself? Or does he mean he would say what he really thinks and feels – if only he could? Is he silenced by overwhelming feelings of pride, fear, inadequacy – and also of knowledge – or is he mute through overwhelming ignorance and misplaced patriotic fervour? He does not actually say. He does not complete his sentences and so all that is certain is that at home he is making himself hoarse with talk which says little of comfort or support.

And the irony is that while all this trivial or tragic 'languaging' is going on – useless, perhaps damaging, words uttered fluently by Lucy, haltingly by mother and father – the soldier in the trenches is silent.

But once more, now filling a noun slot in the phrase 'my self etcetera' and uttered by the narrator himself, *etcetera* is revealing in its ambiguity. Though here – unusually, since it is spoken by the poem's narrator himself and not by one of his family – it may indicate little or nothing. But the emptiness is surely deliberate – and paradoxically meaningful. For what, in this context, could be juxtaposed with the self? Reasons for the war may be debated by those at home. Methods of dying may be preferred. These things may seem important to outsiders but, meanwhile, for the soldier waiting for the battle there is only the self, a self that is physically separated from loved ones and, whoever else is alongside in the mud, alone with his dreams.

As people talked on emptily at home he, himself, was lying quietly in mud – etcetera. Conditions evidently defy all noun fillers except this wryest of understatements. They were no doubt, even if spelled out, beyond the imagining of those at home.

What he was dreaming, etcetera, is parenthetical. But the parenthesis seems an ironic and tragic paradox, for his solitary thoughts and private fantasies are not merely by-the-way, an aside, but no doubt more real than all the talk at home, however well intentioned.

So *etcetera* has the last word and the last laugh. There are only two words important enough in the poem to be capitalized: the final 'Etcetera' is one of them, evidently as vital in its meaning for the speaker as the 'You' whose smile preoccupies him. Hearer/reader response to the word's use on this occasion could vary. Again, as in every other instance of its choosing, our knowledge of language tells us that *etcetera* is 'slotted' into a particular place on the syntagm and so has meaning potential. Again, our experience and knowledge of the world, including this poem, will guide us to fill it in whatever way we can. All the possible nouns for which it could stand would no doubt horrify Aunt Lucy: she would very likely prefer to leave them submerged behind its blandness. For others, this wry *etcetera* might seem, paradoxically, to be so honest that it is the only oblique use of language in the poem that is *not* in some way shocking.

In order for the poem to shock, however, for the complexities and shadows lying behind its frivolous surface to be recognized, cummings must rely on his readers applying the linguistic creativity we all possess. His poem's message must be completed, the implications of all his characters' language choices, including *etcetera*, must be *heard*. It is an obvious point, but noteworthy in relation to everyday language as well as poetry, for the words we choose are not always heard as we would imagine.

HEARING CREATIVITY

As we have already said, all hearers do not respond uniformly to words and structures. Their connotations are not the same for everyone. On the other hand, choices of language are frequently so much a matter of habit that they are taken for granted, hardly heard by their users let alone their hearers, their implications going unchallenged. My attention was drawn to two possible choices of noun to label the police: *service* or *force*. Thinking about it deliberately – much more deliberately than usual – it seems we do not generally speak (although presently there are moves in this direction) of the *police service* and if I use the latter, more usual term, *police force* I, personally, do so automatically, without reflection. But the phrase's possible implications for other hearers become clear when contrasted with emergency telephone procedures. The telephonist has traditionally answered a 999 call with 'Emergency. Which *service*?' If consciously registered, this choice of *service* – to refer to fire, ambulance or police – is a reminder, by contrast, that the more usual *force*, whilst a relatively bland label for some, could connote for other hearers anything but beneficent support.

Not, however, that speakers always want their personal uses and understandings of language, when these do challenge the norm, to be shared. Pejorative heterosexual descriptions of gay and lesbian society have in some cases been taken over by the homosexual community for its own uncensorious use. *Queen*, for instance, in gay usage, loses its abusive edge and becomes acceptable. But homosexual users of such words wish to retain an exclusive right to their own interpretation and usage and do not encourage heterosexual English speakers, however well intentioned, to begin again, join in the retrieval of this vocabulary and share a benign usage. Compromise is resisted because it is just that: a step on the road to unwanted assimilation. Whereas, claiming the offensive vocabulary, and stripping it of its abusive connotations, turns the language back on its original hostile users and maintains difference.

There are parallels here with what Halliday has termed (1978) *anti-languages*. Members of what Halliday calls 'anti-societies' – 'anti' because they are in some sort of antagonistic relationship with the dominant culture – choose to overturn aspects of the language used by the 'norm' society. But, as Fowler points out (1981: 150), the original language is not totally destroyed and replaced. A link with the norm, so-called, is maintained in that traces of the standard remain in some way audible – as they must if the standard is to be openly challenged. Halliday takes some of his examples from Elizabethan vagabond language. Here, an oppositional relationship with the norm society is sometimes articulated through the relexicalization of simple reversal: the leader of a group of criminals is termed *an upright man* and *laws* are methods which must be followed to accomplish crimes successfully.

However, when the goal for innovative language is not merely opposition but involves overturning and replacing the standard, then obviously a whole society must take up the challenging language if the motive behind its introduction is to be achieved. Betty Friedan was one of the first to argue (1963) that there are areas of female experience that have never been 'languaged', making it difficult for women to be heard. Difficult, perhaps, but not impossible (see also chapter 7). For women, using the language creativity available to all, male or female, have been able to produce a number of words and word combinations more acceptable to the women's movement – *chairperson*, *ms*, *date rape* and the like. But these changes do not always receive a sympathetic hearing, let alone usage by society as a whole. Still, even a hostile response is better than none, since ridicule at least takes notice and notice can be a precursor of change.

Neologisms, like *chairperson*, depend as do all elements of language upon structure and rules, this time the rules of morphology. Words are made of morphemes, the smallest meaningful bits, relevant to the whole word, into which they can be divided. *Horses* is therefore two morphemes: *horse* and *s*. The second morpheme, *s*, is meaningful in the sense that it pluralizes *horse*. *Matter*, on the other hand, is only one morpheme. True, *mat* is a syllabic portion of the whole word, and *mat* can have meaning, referring to something like a small rug. But rugs make no sense in the context of the whole word.

Morphemes are not, therefore, the same as syllables which may or may not be meaningful. However, political points have been made through a kind of creativity which stems from combining an intellectual syllabic play with the 'natural' processes of morphology. (It is natural in the sense that it is a rule-governed procedure common to all human language, though manifested in different rules in different languages, acquired and usually practised without deliberate thought. We come to know the morphological rules of our particular language in the manner mentioned above in relation to those children who spot the rule for making past tenses and for a while overextend it to include exceptions to the pattern.)

Herstory and *shero* are feminist examples of this process, deliberately manipulating syllables and morphemes. For neither *his* nor *he* are morphemes in *history* and *hero*. *History* is related to the Greek, *istoria* (and the Greek male pronoun is not *is*). So here creativity depends upon the replacement of a *syllable* with a morpheme. The same is true of *shero*. *Ro* would need to be a morpheme in order to allow *he* morphemic status too, but clearly *ro* has no intrinsic meaning with regard to brave achievers, male or female. Still, the point is made: women take their place in history, a place which is frequently heroic.

Rastafarian language (see Sutcliffe and Wong 1986) is a similar creative challenge – a challenge to conventional unthinking perception and to its automatic 'languaging'. For Rastafarian English also plays between morphology and syllabic division, taking rules to break them in order to practise the spontaneity which, in its expression of feeling, and of clear, fresh thinking, the Rastafarian community prizes. This innovative play with language empowers its users when it substitutes the morpheme *I* for the first morpheme or (like the feminist word play just discussed) the first syllable of a word. *I* is of course a first person pronoun (words are frequently composed of a single morpheme only) and putting it in first place is intended to emphasize the value of a black person in contrast to the worthless invisibility the community feels that black culture has suffered through the white person's racist distancing and dismissal of its invididual members as *you*. So we hear *Iconcile* instead of *reconcile*; *Icreate* instead of *recreate*, *Ispect* instead of *respect*. And because the syllable *ate* sounds harsh, and in any case is reminiscent of the morpheme *hate*, it will probably be replaced. *Congregate/congregation* may become *congrelove* but, given Rastafarian refusal to be linguistically limited, another speaker might choose to say *congregman* instead of *congregation* – but not *congremen*. The morpheme *man* is acceptable whilst *men* is not because the Son of Man brought good to the world whereas men are fallen in sin.

We cannot fail to hear and react to such unconventional creativity. Besides, Rastafarian speakers, intending their language to be noticed, use its sound and rhythm patterns to draw attention to their messages. But significant invention is not always so open and honest. Our knowledge of structural manoeuvres, and of paradigmatic choice along the syntagmatic chain, permits a way with words that, because it may not be consciously heard, even by its speaker, wields an insidious power. In this respect linguists (see for example Kress and Hodge 1979: 15–37) have pointed out the relevance of the concept of 'transformation', the idea (based on the original 'classical' Chomskyan syntactic model of 1957 and 1965) that the words we utter and receive are only the 'surface' structure of language which, lying unheard in a 'deeper' structure, may have clearer and more disturbing implications than the blander words we actually hear.

Nominalization is an example of this phenomenon: it is as if whole underlying clauses have been reduced to nouns, losing in the process all reference to action and actors. For instance, the first noun phrase in the sentence **Political correctness** *sweeps American campuses* – or even **PCism** *sweeps American campuses* – is a distillation of something like *Certain political ideas are deemed correct by certain people*. True, the phrase or word may be spoken with deliberate irony by opponents of the movement in order to mock the 'multiculturalism' which claims to give a rational hearing to previously ignored minorities. But, by masking the existence and activity of human instigators – and therefore, given their humanness, the fallibility of their philosophy, the possibility of *in*correctness – the simple phrase, whoever speaks it, can help to give authority to the movement.

And the movement may or may not warrant its power and authority. Without investigating its supporters' language – just as they recommend the language of others be investigated for hidden and destructive ideology – it is impossible to know. Unless we actively interpret the words that are chosen to make up the chains of human language we shall be bound by those chains.

It is this active participation in the languaging of our selves and our experiences of the world that 'etcetera' demands. cummings' poem speaks of war, but it also reminds us of the power that is language, a power possessed by all, yet not always consciously, or conscientiously, turned to account.

SUGGESTIONS FOR FURTHER WORK

1 Readers who would like to extend this brief introduction to aspects of language, including its structure and its acquisition, would find texts like Aitchison 1987 and 1989 very helpful. Those who wish to pursue syntactic metalanguage would find Crystal (1988) useful.

2 cummings' poem 'anyone lived in a pretty how town' (Firmage 1981: 515) makes highly unusual syntactic and semantic choices. What words, given your unconsciously acquired, creative knowledge of English, would you have expected to find in their places? How does your knowledge of 'normal' English help you to make sense of cummings' unusual selections?

3 Identify nominalizations in examples of media language. Work out their unstated implications. Having done so, does your understanding of/ reaction to the texts in which you found them alter significantly?

3 Sound and meaning
'The upper birch-leaves' by Thomas Hardy

The following chapter considers the implications of Thomas Hardy's poem and also, with particular reference to English, the part that may be played by phonetic segments (vowels and consonants) and suprasegmental language features (particularly intonation, stress and rhythm) in the signalling of meaning.

The upper birch-leaves

Warm yellowy-green	1
In the blue serene,	
How they skip and sway	
On this autumn day!	4
They cannot know	
What has happened below, –	
That their boughs down there	
Are already quite bare,	8
That their own will be	
When a week has passed, –	
For they jig as in glee	
To this very last.	12

But no; there lies	
At times in their tune	
A note that cries	
What at first I fear	16
I did not hear:	
'O we remember	
At each wind's hollo –	
Though life holds yet –	20
We go hence soon,	
For tis November;	

– But that *you* follow
You may forget!'   24
   (Gibson 1976: 507)

Thomas Hardy's poem, 'The upper birch-leaves', is, first and foremost, about intimations of mortality, intimations which human beings, especially the young, might prefer not to acknowledge. It implies that the inescapable fact of death is known to everyone – after all, death is observed terminating the lives of the sick and elderly – yet this is a truth that may be ignored by the young and healthy, for it seems to have little to do with their own vitality.

Hardy uses an image of leaves and branches in order to make the point. These are personified. The upper leaves are dancing happily it seems, apparently relishing their vigour at the top of the tree. But, as they do so, other leaves are falling from the lower boughs beneath them. To the watching persona, speaking in stanza 1, the upper birch-leaves seem ignorant that they too will soon suffer the same fate as those lower down.

But this observer is mistaken. Although the leaves dance, apparently feeling secure and enjoying life to the full, even these upper ones are, at some level of consciousness, aware of their own impending death. It is an awareness that the observer notices only later. Perhaps s/he has preferred not to recognize a self-knowledge in the leaves which might force a parallel acknowledgement of his or her own human mutability.

In order to explain this Hardy refers to sound, to the meaningful 'tune' of the leaves as it is heard by the listener. He writes,

. . . there lies
At times in their tune
A note that cries
What at first I fear
I did not hear:

That 'note' cries out the leaves' inevitable fate – and ours. 'We birch-leaves', it signals, 'sometimes acknowledge that we must die – but you who watch us, presently enjoying strength and vigour like ourselves, may forget that your own living takes its toll and you too will die.'

But Hardy not only *refers* to sound to make this point. He also *uses* it: through it he demonstrates a human reluctance to face unwelcome messages by causing readers to experience sound signals whose disturbing significance we may, either through insensitivity or resistance, fail at first to hear.

And so, whilst this poem is essentially about mortality, it is also at a secondary level about language, reminding us that we do not always hear the complex signals of sounds, whatever their message may be.

These sounds are of different sorts. It can be helpful to think of two tiers. On one tier there are *segments*, vowels and consonants, that form up into words. Then there is a tier of *suprasegmental* features, including intonation (based on pitch), stress and rhythm: suprasegmental features are aspects of what is also called 'prosody', the term extending beyond its reference to metrical patterns in literature. But the notion of tiers is metaphorical for, in practice, the two kinds of sound fuse together to composite effect, conveying meaning that includes indications of emotion, attitude, syntactic meaning, 'information structure' and so on. In addition there are *paralinguistic* sound features, qualities of voice – like huskiness – which may be less central to the conveying of meaning than segments and suprasegmental indicators.

What follows immediately is a general discussion of English sound and meaning. This will then be related to 'The upper birch-leaves'.

ENGLISH SOUND AND MEANING

The phonetic segments of spoken language

Consonant sounds are made when the flow of air is obstructed by the tongue or lips as it passes through the mouth. Vowels are made when there is no such oral obstruction.

Individual vowels and consonants do not usually (except when they form whole words, like *I* or *a*) have semanticity: they do not carry intrinsic meaning. They can, however, signal the *presence* of meaning. For, if we change the first consonant of *tray* to produce *fray* we are talking about something quite different. Different meaning is also signalled if we change the vowel of *tray* and say *tree*. The contrasts in these pairs confirm that (using International Phonetic Alphabet symbols) /t/, /f/, /ei/ and /i/ are significant sounds. And because they can affect meaning in this sort of way they, together with other phonetic segments which are similarly important in English, are referred to as *phonemes*.

Difference and contrast are basic to the communicative structures of language. As the Swiss linguist, Ferdinand de Saussure (1857–1913) pointed out (Bally, Sechehaye and Reidlinger 1964: 88–9), language is in a number of ways like a game of chess and this analogy is pursued here. We can play chess traditionally with carved ivory figures. But if we find ourselves shipwrecked on to a desert island, and our carved figures of pawns, rooks and so on have gone down with the ship, all is not lost. We could carry on playing by using pebbles found on the beach. The crucial thing is that the pebbles must contrast with each other in some way. Then, those of us playing must agree that one particular shape, or perhaps colour, of pebble 'means' the king. We must agree that another, a different shape or colour, means the queen, and so on. Alternatively we could choose fragments of wood – just so long as these contrast with each other and so long as we all agree what the differences in shape, or texture, or colour mean.

It is important to note that the correspondence between the features of the pebbles, or wood, and what we want them to mean is *arbitrary*. It is the same with language. The English choice of the word *tree* is arbitrary. It is not selected because it has any obvious link with forests. As we say the word its vowels and consonants do not sound, or feel in the mouth anything like a thing with trunk, branches and leaves. We could just as easily have called it a *siz* or a *blup*. German has chosen *Baum*, French has arbitrarily picked *arbre*, and so on. There is no similarity between any of these words, and none between them and the object they signify.

There is of course an exception to this general rule. There are onomatopoeic words, so called because they do have resemblance. For example, *quack* or *crackle* (and perhaps – see chapter 1 – Lok's choice of 'kwak' to refer to the ravens) are examples of onomatopoeia because they do sound something like the noise to which they refer.

We might take this further. A nineteenth-century poet, William Barnes, was convinced that the vowel sounds of his native Dorset, being 'mellower' (1847: 48) than those outside the county, were a reflection of his neighbours' gentle, friendly natures. But this could hardly have been indisputably true. The way people 'sound' their language can, certainly, be an indication of their individual or cultural personalities, and Barnes' Dorset vowels were often, partly because of certain other language features (see chapter 6), lengthy and slowly pronounced. But, as John Lyons points out, 'cultural and linguistic differences must be independently identifiable before they can be correlated' (1977: 249–50). Unless we have something else to go on, some other evidence of behaviour, it would be unwise to assume that everyone we meet with a pleasing set of vowels is charming and kind!

Still, we might agree with Barnes that certain sounds can seem soft, round, 'mellow', even if it does not automatically follow that their users are gentle souls. (Our agreement with Barnes may depend upon our sharing a similar cultural background. Speakers of a different language, from a different culture, might associate different implications with such sounds.) Other sound segments can seem to us sharp, harsh, clipped. For example, although each of us might choose alternative words to describe our interpretation, in principle we would very likely agree that *ruby* sounds quite different from *grit* – perhaps richer, less sharp, less unattractively tinny. As it happens, our contrasting judgement of these two words is appropriate since the one is a thing of beauty and value, the other comparatively worthless and unaesthetic. But of course such correlations do not always hold true. There does not seem (to my ear) anything particularly unattractive, hard or awkward, about the sound of the word *tumour*. On the contrary: even though it has a particularly unpleasant denotation, the word rolls easily from the tongue, flows gently through the lips. However, when a correlation between sound and meaning does exist, it can reinforce the significance of a word for speaker and hearer.

In any event, the meanings we derive, in whatever way, from groups of segments, are generally augmented by 'suprasegmental' features. These are clearly heard in spoken language, but may also be supplied to our mind's ear as we silently read.

Suprasegmental and paralinguistic features

Suprasegmental features, so called because they affect more than one segment and, including intonation, stress and tempo are also, together with paralinguistic features, 'sound effects' of significance.

Intonation involves *pitch*, high or low, made by the vibration of the vocal cords and carried by vowel sounds. The faster the vibration, the higher the pitch. Pitch can also be 'contoured', gliding from high to low, low to high.

A very large number of languages – including Chinese, many native American languages, and more than a thousand African languages – are called *tone languages* because some of their words can each have a number of quite different meanings depending on their chosen pitch. For instance, in Kono (a West African language) *bu*, spoken with a relatively high pitch, means 'horn', but, spoken with a relatively low pitch, it means 'to be cross'. In some languages using a different pitch *contour* across a word will alter its meaning. If you allowed the tone of *naa* to fall from high to low it would, in the Thai language, mean 'face'. But if you let it rise, from low to high, it would mean 'thick'.

English is not one of these tone languages. Pitching the English word *cat* relatively high or low, or gliding its tone from one to the other, will never make it mean something entirely different, like 'word-processor' or 'to navigate'.

But pitch still matters in English. English is called an *intonational language* because its contours of pitch, changing from low to high, or vice versa, across a stretch of language, will produce a rising or falling melody of intonation. This, in conjunction with other suprasegmental features like stress and tempo, whilst not altering the fundamental definitions of our words, can indicate meaning of various kinds, including grammatical, emotional and indexical meaning: it can also be an indication of what is called 'information structure'.

With regard to **grammatical meaning** and intonation, if we taste a glass of wine and say *This is vintage* with a falling or a rise–fall tone on its last word, we are probably making a firm, approving statement. But say it with rising, or fall–rise intonation on these last two syllables and instead of making a statement we are indicating a question without having to alter the syntactic form. (A notation for describing intonation is suggested below in suggestions for further work (1).)

As for **emotional meaning**, this question could – particularly if spoken by a wine connoisseur – be one that registers surprise, maybe ironic surprise, even angry disbelief. Other sound factors would help to confirm or deny these possibilities. For example, by increasing the volume on a particular syllable, or changing its pitch, or making it longer, or by choosing some combination of these three variables, we produce *stress*. Stress is meaningful in a number of ways, including the attitudinal. A degree of emphasis upon the first syllable of *vintage* could add to the emotional content of the sentence: the greater the stress, the greater the amazed horror: *This is vintage?*

Tempo is another suprasegmental feature. Speaking quickly may convey urgency. Querying the wine's vintage slowly might sound disconcertingly menacing.

Pitch, stress and tempo are involved in the production of *rhythm*. English uses a *stress-timed* rhythm, stressing syllables at fairly regular intervals with unstressed syllables in between. Stress is of course integral to poetic metre. But stress is internalized as we acquire language whilst metre is learned separately, its regularities a constraint imposed on the language, sometimes coinciding with everyday, non-literary stress, sometimes not.

Pauses in rhythm can also be significant in the English expression of attitude. A small gap between *this* and *is* could turn a mild query about the wine's quality into one of amazement, even despair. Silence can be as potent as sound. We enjoy 'comfortable' silences and dislike 'threatening' silences.

Another kind of meaning, apart from the grammatical and the emotional or attitudinal, is related to the **information structure** of an utterance. Sound effects help to indicate what is already known, or 'given', in a remark and what is quite 'new'. If prominence is given to *vintage* it may be assumed that the wine, but not its quality, has been mentioned recently. Conversely, if *this* is emphasized, then quality has been the subject of conversation, not – until this moment – the particular glass you are drinking.

Sound effects can also have meaning of an *indexical* kind. They can, for instance, indicate membership of a social group. If we hear English used with certain kinds of suprasegmental indicators we know we are at the races, listening to a bookmaker. Other sound signals would confirm that we are in a church listening to a minister.

Apart from the suprasegmental aspects of sound there are also *paralinguistic* features (so called because they may be less central to the conveyance of meaning) based on the *timbre* or 'quality' of the voice. Husky-sounding speech may, for instance, suggest deep emotion.

All in all, 'sound effects' are profoundly meaningful. Without them the communicative power of speakers would be radically reduced (the silent signing of the deaf includes alternative hand and body indicators) and to utter groups of words entirely *without* rhythm and intonation is extremely difficult – more robotic than human.

In fact, we start to imitate intonation patterns as babies of around eight months, soon after reaching the babbling stage. Different languages clearly sound quite distinct in a broad sort of way and we seem able to identify our own language's particular patterns. French babies as young as four days old were observed behaving differently when French was being spoken around them from when hearing English or Italian (Mehler *et al.*: 1988). They sucked more strongly on pacifiers and since babies suck at higher rates when roused and interested it is suggested that they may have begun to notice and become acclimatized to their parents' sound patterns in the womb.

But though languages sound broadly distinct one from the other, they are all selecting and adapting from a very similar set of possible suprasegmental and paralinguistic features, yet when two languages choose the same feature they may not mean the same thing by it at all. If a marriage proposal leaves its English recipient silent, an English suitor would be disappointed. But if your would-be husband is Japanese, your lack of comment would count as acceptance! The timbre of the voice has a different message in different places too. Breathy voices on English telephones may be treated with suspicion; in Japan they may convey respect!

They *may*. But it is not possible to be dogmatic. There is a large degree of flexibility and considerable complexity about the signalling of meaning through sound, particularly attitudinal meaning. To tell a foreign speaker how to express dismay, or fear, or anger, or love, through the available sound signals of English is problematic because there are no hard and fast rules, particularly since, as we have already noted, we imply what we mean through a package deal of interrelating intonation, stress, tempo, pause and so on. Experience will tell the learner that sometimes a rising intonation can 'mean' a question. But sometimes it means fear. Sometimes it means a warning. Sometimes it means passion. Its final interpretation, by a hearer, depends on associated sound signals and of course the context of the utterance.

This uncertainty and vagueness surrounding the implications of sound is not, as Labov and Fanshel point out with specific regard to intonation (1977: 46), necessarily a disadvantage.

Speakers need a form of communication which is *deniable*. It is advantageous for them to express hostility, challenge the competence of others, or express friendliness and affection in a way that can be denied if they are explicitly held to account for it. If there were not such a deniable channel of communication, and intonational contours became so well recognized and explicit that people were accountable for their intonation, then some other mode of deniable communication would undoubtedly develop.

Moreover, if the sound signals of an utterance are in some way disconcerting it can be advantageous, not only for a speaker but also for a hearer, to be able to deny what has been heard. Even if I believe I have expressed my preference as strongly as my control of intonation and the like allows, the sentence *I wish you would stop smoking* might still be heard by an addict as an expression of mild preference rather than of deep concern.

And the mistake need not be one of deliberate self-deception. Hearers may not be able to interpret signals of sound with absolute certainty because their combinations are so subtle and complex. For one thing, the sounds may be delivering a 'mixed message'. It is perfectly possible for words and syntax to say one thing but to seem to the hearer at odds with suprasegmental and paralinguistic features. Sarcasm is expressed in this sort of way, but its message is usually clear because the overriding aspect of sound meaning is generally given prominence. Yet there is likely to be confusion if I say *I wish you would give up smoking* and sound relatively cheerful. Do the suprasegmental indicators carry a message stronger than the words themselves: do I not really mind? Or is it just that I want to avoid an argument?

As for the much more profound message of Hardy's upper birch-leaves, it is certainly complex – and mixed. The second stanza clarifies the position, but its observer begins by discounting the poem's 'notes' probably because of their subtlety and perhaps because of their disconcerting significance. The reader of the poem is in a similar position.

THE SOUNDS OF 'THE UPPER BIRCH-LEAVES'

I have already suggested that Hardy actually uses sound to allow the reader to *experience* what he means. That is, he not only tells us that we may ignore what we do not wish to acknowledge, forget what we do not choose to remember ('But that *you* follow/You may forget'), he also emphasizes our deliberate or unconscious self-deception – and at the same time makes a secondary point about language – by inviting us to discover for ourselves how we can be deaf to messages in the 'notes' that are apparently sounded by the leaves as they move in the breeze. For if we are not reading – listening – carefully, not only Hardy's persona but we ourselves may not at first acknowledge their disconcerting warning. Yet these notes, like the truth they signal, were always there for the hearing in the language Hardy chooses to describe the behaviour of the leaves – just as messages of various kinds are there in the sound effects we hear in everyday language.

Reading carefully is of course much the same as listening carefully, because even if we are reading silently we have to supply to our mind's ear the kind of sound effects that would be there in an audible reading. Otherwise we are without the intonation and so forth that we need in order to complete and clarify meaning.

On occasion, of course, words on the page leave us considerable freedom in hearing their prosodic tier. Even Shakespeare's principal characters can sometimes be interpreted in more than one way. For example, Ronald Chan suggests (unpublished material, Loughborough University of Technology English and Drama Department) that, depending on his understanding of the whole play, an actor can, through the suprasegmental and paralinguistic signals he selects, make Shylock in his *Merchant of Venice* speech beginning 'To bait fish withal – if it will feed nothing else it will feed my revenge' (III.i.47–66), either impassioned and vengeful or dignified and logical.

In other instances, however, the structuring of a written utterance will guide and limit choices of interpretation. Hardy himself takes advantage of the special features conventionally available to poetry – for example, rhyme and marked rhythm – to encourage a particular reading of 'The upper birch-leaves'.

The effect of the poem is, naturally, the effect of the *whole*. Each line, each syntactic structure, each word and sound and rhythm, works with every other signal to make, particularly on reflection, a composite impact. But the reader/listener has to begin at the beginning, hearing the poem line by line, one signal after the other. And if it is read in entirety and without particular scrutiny, a first response may be achieved that is as unselfconscious and spontaneous as possible – putting the reader in much the same position as the poem's persona, listening to the birch-leaves for the first time.

However, even at a first uncritical reading, a difference is likely to be noticed between the two stanzas. Several readers of the poem have told me that, for them, it is harder to read, and certainly to articulate, the second stanza than the first. The likely reasons for this become clear as attention is paid, on a subsequent reading, to each line and to the effect of the whole. The poem invites this second, more careful reading when its persona acknowledges that there was, recorded in the first stanza, a crucial note sounded by the leaves that 'cries' what at first s/he fears s/he did not hear.

The first signficant note I hear especially clearly, on a critical second reading at least, is segmental: the vowel sound of the first rhyming couplet, the phoneme /i/ in *green* and *serene*. Its very repetition makes it noticeable. But, in addition, suprasegmental factors combine to draw attention to it; for instance, the rhythm of each line 'punches' a small stress onto these closing vowels. Moreover, there seems to be a brief pause after each line which helps to draw more attention to their final sounds than would have been the case if they had run on, the first glancing over its rhyming vowel and flowing without pause into the second, the second merging into the third.

To me, this rhymed /i/ – in this particular context – has a pleasing quality. It sounds to be drawn out, with nothing jarring or disturbing about it and easy articulation of these final vowels, lingered over in their slight stressing, seems to give a small sensation of pleasant relaxation. Of course this is a personal judgement. But it is, I think, a judgement endorsed by the first four lines' composite image of clear and sensuous detail. We are directly told that the leaves are a warm yellowy green and the sky is peacefully blue: soft and pretty colours (though see a qualification made below) in a tranquil atmosphere.

It is no wonder the leaves are contentedly skipping and swaying in such an atmosphere. And the reader can share their experience, for the regular, easy rhythm of the first four lines, with fairly brisk tempo, actually mimics the leaves' movements, giving a sense of their swaying, jigging dance. There are two main stresses in each of these lines and it is appropriate that their dancing rhythm should fall on the words 'skip' and 'sway', drawing attention to these activities.

There is one other tiny sound clue in lines 3 and 4. The vowel sounds of 'sway' and 'day', emphasized by the rhythm are – given this relaxed scenario – appropriately free and easy to say, not clipped by a rapidly following or hard-sounding consonant. All in all, then, the sound signals of these first four lines, segments and suprasegmental features, not only describe a situation but combine to let the reader *sense* the leaves' apparently carefree happiness. The simple, easy rhythms, clear and mellow sounds, have a nursery-rhyme feel.

The next two lines, 5 and 6, have a similar rhythm to this first batch of four and, again, there seems to be a brief pause between them. They, too, rhyme neatly and it is also true that the closing vowel sounds of 'know' and 'below', like the rhyming phonemes of the introductory lines, could not in any way be described as harsh. But is there a mixed message here? For, despite these pleasant and regular sound effects, the words themselves carry a hint of disturbance: just what is it 'they cannot know'?

The next couplet explains, and though lines 7 and 8 have much in common with their predecessors – maintaining, for instance, a steady beat – there is a small but significant sound difference in line 7 which reinforces the image and import of the bare boughs. Given the very different message of the words in lines 4–8 – a message no longer of carefree play but now of decay on the lower boughs – it is not surprising that it is a disruptive, jarring difference. Up to now all the lines have been extremely easy to say. But there is, I suggest, something physically awkward about articulating line 7:

That their boughs down there

In my experience many readers find it hard to repeat *th*, /ð/, at the beginning of the first two and the last words. It can be awkward because it is necessary to keep pushing the tongue between the teeth to form this appropriately named 'interdental' sound. In addition, 'boughs' and 'down' begin with consonants. The first, /b/, is a 'bilabial', so named because it is made by pushing the lips together. The second, /d/, is an 'alveolar' because it is made by raising the tip of the tongue to the bony tooth ridge, the alveolar ridge. So there are a lot of acrobatics going on in the mouth, letting air out, holding it in, and rapidly shunting the tongue around the mouth in order to do so. Of course, by definition, there are always acrobatics going on in speech: sounds are made in this way. And it is not that /ð/, /b/ or /d/ are especially difficult in themselves to pronounce (after all, 'the' was not hard work in line 2, and nor was 'they' in line 5) but the clustering together of consonants, one or other at the start of each and every monosyllabic word in line 7, gives a slightly clumsy feel to it, making its words uncomfortably noticeable. (The beginning of line 9 is similar).

Still, as we have said, up to this point the stanza has tripped along in neatly rhyming couplets: skipped and swayed along like the upper birch-leaves themselves, even through the 'difficult' phonemes and other small hints of warning in lines 4–8. The rhymes continue to be neat and easy in lines 9–12, and the rhythm continues to jig along, like the leaves, 'to this very last'. However, the rhyme is now made between alternate lines: 'be/glee', 'passed/last'. So the pattern is different from what has gone before – and difference, especially when it disrupts an extremely regular, secure pattern of any kind, in art or in life, can be disconcerting.

However, whilst readers of this chapter may agree with this last sentence and with my description of the poem's sounds in general, they may still feel my responses to them are all too subjective to count, the differences too slight to be meaningful or the significance I am attaching to them too far-fetched. After all, poetry is, for instance, littered with neatly rhyming couplets which do not, in themselves, signal meanings of 'security'. And altering their pattern does not always invite speculation about disconcerting anxieties.

But I have already suggested that stanza 2 gives my responses credence. It confirms the importance of stanza 1's sound effects, encouraging the reader not to dismiss them, not to leave them unnoticed – in the same way that sound signals in everyday language use may be ignored or misconstrued – but instead to listen again and to give them due weight. It confirms that in the tune of this first verse there do lie 'notes' which the reader, like the poem's persona watching and listening to the leaves, may not at first have heard, notes that disturb the equilibrium. Stanza 2 tells us directly that this is so – and also demonstrates the fact.

Everything about its sound and rhythm is different in contrast with the sound and rhythm of stanza 1. It has already been suggested that it is rather more difficult to read this second stanza than the first one. All through the first verse there were regularly stressed lines, without internal breaks, which did not run on, and a neat rhyme scheme (albeit changing) of aa,bb,cc,dd,efef. Now this pattern is disrupted.

The stanza starts with an arresting caesura, a major 'cut' in the line. The first phrase before the caesura is short and sharp, two mono-syllables abruptly terminated, with an explosive /b/ to begin the exclamation and probably a falling tone to close it. It is tempting to say 'no' loudly and emphatically, and if we have been lulled along with the swaying leaves – content like they appear to be, deaf to threatening signals, not reacting to the hints of tricky phrases and altered sound patterns in stanza 1 – we now have to pay attention. This brief introductory phrase pulls us up short and the reader must listen carefully and accept that

> . . . there lies
> At times in their tune
> A note that cries
> What at first I fear
> I did not hear

That meaningful note was always there, in the 'tune' of stanza 1, had we been alert to it. It was there, for instance, in the awkwardness of *th*, and the change of rhyme scheme just marginally disturbing the secure regularity of stanza 1's form.

The lines following stanza 2's arresting introduction continue to make sure we will pay attention now. There are two main stresses in lines 13–17, just as there were in the first four of the first verse, but this time the reader is not encouraged to imagine swaying in time with them. These lines run on, one after the other, the consonant at the end of each for the most slipping easily into a vowel at the start of the next. The tongue has no trouble here. On the contrary: it cannot stop. The tempo seems to me to increase and, as the lines speed on, I feel the pitch rise, up and up. Yet it is also possible to read these lines with sinking intonation. Each reader will make a personal decision. But I am tempted to a rising intonational curve probably because it echoes the mounting anxiety that the words themselves – about a 'crying' note and 'fear' – appear to suggest.

Besides, the security of a consistent rhyme pattern has gone in stanza 2. There are, to be sure, six rhymed pairs of lines. But these do not follow each other in any particular order. Instead we get a scheme – if, in its irregularity, you can call it a scheme – of abaccdefbdef. Disruption of rhyme pattern is now the norm – and even this sound effect is appropriate to the meaning of the poem since the disruption of life, a constant insecurity between the two fixed points of birth and death, is the normal human condition.

The last seven lines of the poem make this truth plain. The leaves speak: 'We go hence soon'. We might have known it even in the first line of the poem. For though the leaves jigged along happily then, 'warmly' coloured a 'yellow green', green that has yellowed is a green that is decaying. And, now, finality and gravity are clearly dramatized in appropriately end-stopped lines with ponderous stresses that slow the reader down. But where, precisely, should these stresses fall? The placing of two main stresses in earlier lines was not in doubt but now there is some confusion, a number of possibilities, so whilst the words of these final lines are unambiguous in their meaning, there is, appropriately, nothing glib and easy in their delivery.

In these last phrases, for the first time, the poem makes explicit the connection between the metaphor of the personified leaves and humanity. Hardy uses typography, italicizing *you* so that the reader cannot miss hearing the most important stresses of the poem. And punctuation, the use of an exclamation mark at the very end of the poem, also invites the reader to hear in the sounds, rhythms and intonation of the final couplet, the urgency, irony and seriousness of the message.

> – But that *you* follow
> You may forget!

AN EVERYDAY ART

All in all, then, it seems to me indisputable that there is a match between the sounds of 'The upper birch-leaves' and its theme of ignored, or ambiguous, intimations of mortality. But I have also been arguing, of course, that the subtlety of the poem's messages, and the complexity of reader response to them, make meaningful sound and its reception in everyday language an additional theme of the poem. This theme can be demonstrated so clearly because, whilst the language of poetry is not of course utterly distinct from naturally occurring utterances, it is able to draw attention to significances of sound by using the marked patterns, especially of rhyme and rhythm, that can be amongst its defining features.

I am not insisting that Thomas Hardy consciously and meticulously plotted every aspect of the sound and rhythm of 'The upper birch-leaves'. And any poem may have for its readers meanings that were not imagined by its creator. But I am inclined to think this is a very deliberately crafted and focused poem. After all, Hardy did define art as 'a changing of the actual proportions and order of things ... to show more clearly the features that matter in those realities, which, if merely copied or reported inventorially, might possibly be observed, but would more probably be overlooked' (F.E. Hardy 1962: 228–9). To this end he was skilled in blending the natural speaking voice with the more stylized articulation of poetry, evidently recognizing and making the most of sound's capacity to mean.

Certainly, not only 'The upper birch-leaves' but all Hardy's poetry emphasizes the truism that reading poetry means listening carefully. The same careful attention to the significance of sound is required for all language, including the everyday, if its segmental and suprasegmental resources are to be fully utilized, heard and understood. Making sound sense, as it were, is an everyday art.

SUGGESTIONS FOR FURTHER WORK

1 *Notation*

It is helpful in describing intonation to use a conventional notation. Haynes (1989: 108–14) explains and develops the following method in detail. Utterances may be divided into *tone units*, marked off by *tone boundaries*, each unit including a *tone nucleus*, or *tonic syllable*, a point at which pitch moves. This movement in pitch (perhaps accompanied by a lengthened sound, or increased volume) comes over to the hearer as stress. There may also be a lesser stress in the tone unit. If so, it comes before the nucleus and carries *key*, the level from which pitch movement, when it occurs at the nucleus, is felt to begin. Try articulating the following examples, guided by the notation, and assess the kind of meaning you are conveying thereby. Double slanted lines mark tone boundaries. The lines above words show the direction of intonation movement. Bold capitals indicate primary stress. Ordinary capitals show the lesser stress of key.

(a) // This is **VÌN**tage //
(b) // **THÌS** is **VÌN**tage //
(c) // This **ÌS** vintage //
(d) // THIS is **VÌN**tage //

2 The following two verses offer very different images of autumn: the first emphasizes autumn's mature beauty; the second stresses its decay. The difference is signalled not simply through words, but also through sound and rhythm. Try describing these differences of sound and rhythm and suggest how they contribute to the contrast of meaning.

(a)

> This golden autumn's tawny leaves
> Glow and gleam in the setting sun.

(b)

> Their dying autumn colder grows.
> Its drying leaves fall and fade.
> They lie and die, torn and brown,
> Scuffed on the mud-caked earth.

3 Try, as suggested in this chapter, reading Shylock's *Merchant of Venice* speech beginning 'To bait fish withal' (III.i.47–66) in a number of ways. Carefully describe your different choices of intonation, pace, stress and so on, explaining what you intend them to mean. Do those listening to you hear the same meanings?

4 Imagine you are at a football match. Try registering your different attitudes and emotions when your team, and then the opposing one, scores. Stick to the same words whichever team is scoring: *What a goal*. Then, whatever variations you make to indicate your pleasure or your distress will hang on intonation, stress, pause and rhythm. Ask people in the group with you to listen carefully, describe the variations you make, and then check with you to see if their interpretation of them matches your own intentions.

4 Making meaning
Susan Sontag's essay 'AIDS and its metaphors' and Eva Salzman's poem 'Time out'

This chapter develops a number of themes that were briefly discussed in chapter 1. With reference to Lakoff and Johnson's Metaphors We Live By *(1980) it relates some implications of the Sapir–Whorf hypothesis to the liberating and limiting selection of words and of metaphors.*

'IMAGINE THERE BEING NO EXACTING WORD FOR TIME'

The Sapir–Whorf hypothesis argues that we are to some extent *determined* by our language in a *culturally relative* way. Edward Sapir, the American anthropologist, believed that our particular society's world 'is to a large extent unconsciously built up on the language habits of the group' (Sapir 1929, reprinted in Mandelbaum 1949: 160). In the even more deterministic view of Benjamin Lee Whorf, who had been Sapir's pupil, language is 'the shaper of ideas' so that 'no individual is free to describe nature with absolute impartiality but is constrained to certain modes of interpretation even while he thinks himself most free'. Therefore, to his way of thinking, people cannot be 'led by the same physical evidence to the same picture of the universe, unless their linguistic backgrounds are similar or in some way can be calibrated' (Carroll and Wiley 1956: 214).

Put very simply, and at its most extreme, the hypothesis implies that, if a particular language does not have ready-made words for something, its speakers cannot know that 'something' – but a speaker of a different language, which does include relevant words and structures, can and, indeed, must.

Consider this in the context of English. The language identifies *time*. Are its speakers obliged, then, determined by the word and its uses, to adopt Whorf's 'certain modes of interpretation' – possibly interpretations we might prefer to do without? Moreover, would English speakers be constrained to see the world differently if the language had no such word? Do speakers of other languages, which appear not to have a similar term, inevitably perceive a different world than we do?

We might try, with Eva Salzman in her poem 'Time out' (quoted in full at the end of this chapter), to 'Imagine there being no exacting word for time' (Rumens 1992: 62). Perhaps then, as Salzman suggests, there would be

> . . . nothing to waste or save, invent
> or slip away.

But, in the absence of 'time', what alternatives, of language and perception, would present themselves instead? Perhaps, if we were without the word, and others associated with it, we should not think of duration or of specific, cyclical moments but instead

> . . . take, say, the three-cigarette
>
> train departing half-past-after-the-last-word
> which wants saying (and not a moment too soon!)
> while the numberless dial of my watch would refer
> to a changing mise-en-scène winding from sun to moon.

This might be a blessed relief, for in this case

> . . . I wouldn't think to worry if I were late
> for anything, wouldn't care by when which boat
> came in.

And it would certainly seem, in the apparently minuteless, hourless world of this new English, that

> . . . tides
> aren't for living by, but are only there to admire
> occasionally on trips to the timeless sea-sides.

Yet of course, if tides are admired they have been noted – even without the language and the concept of 'time'. And the moon has been seen to wax and wane, the sun to rise and set. Still, even so, observers might not be obliged to 'time' their movements, labelling minutes, hours and days. The same sun and moon were visible in the sky above the American Hopi Indian, on whose language Whorf based much of his thinking. But the Hopi language does not appear to label separate segments of time, minutes, hours, days. Instead its grammatical struc-tures seem to identify ongoing processes. Whilst we perceive, measure and count seconds and minutes, days and months, the Hopi appears to image a kind of 'flow' of 'time' in which things have occurred, are occurring or may yet occur – but not at specifically identified moments, separated out from the flow.

Nevertheless, given a particular style of life in the world of tides and sun and moon, surely an idea of precise timing would follow? Supposing I were, as Salzman writes, to

> . . . say to friends:
> 'I'll meet you at the end of this cooking of rice'
> or, more vaguely still: 'You know . . . when the afternoon ends.'
> When? Would I be on time, guided by a smoky feel of night,
> when it fell, in my bones – another made-up clocking-in machine?

It seems very likely. However, lacking ready-made language to label a 'made-up clocking-in machine', there might be a problem, at least for a while:

> . . . how would I measure these purposeful distances run,
> or almost run, as the case would more likely seem?
> The racers might just laugh or chat at the starting-gun.

But language could soon be found to label the distinctions we had experienced and found important. As Sapir himself noted: people who had never before seen a horse 'were compelled to invent or borrow a word for the animal when they made his acquaintance' (1921: 219).

There would be no difficulty in this. The capacity for creativity is a defining feature of human language (see chapter 2). Given morphological rules, we can derive new words from old, adding suffixes, prefixes or compounding. And completely fresh neologisms are perfectly possible.

However, the invention of new words is not our only creative ploy. An alternative way to develop and communicate our fresh perceptions is, of course, through metaphor, utilizing existing language and concepts, borrowing terms that usually refer to something quite different but are in some way relevant for our new purpose. It is a linguistic feat accomplished by all of us, all of the time and with such impact that Lakoff and Johnson entitle their book on the subject *Metaphors We Live By* and contend that our 'ordinary conceptual system, in terms of which we both think and act, is fundamentally metaphorical in nature' (1980: 3). For instance, when we talk (as we do, day in day out) about argument as if it were a battle – *I won, you lost, I shot down your every point* – we are talking metaphor. Say, *Her ego is fragile, She goes to pieces at the slightest thing, She'll snap if you push her*, and we are using metaphor, seeing the mind in terms of a brittle object.

Indeed, to return to the theme of Salzman's poem, we are in the realm of metaphor if we take that everyday word *time* and say we *waste* it, or *save* it, or *spend* it, because in so doing we are borrowing language from another area, in this case the money market. The perception seems accurate enough since, in our culture (though maybe not in the Hopi's with its concentration on process rather than entities), it is our experience that time, whilst not a tangible commodity like pounds and pence, *is* in some sense, money. We are paid by the hour, the week, the month; and deadlines missed are orders lost and jobs jeopardized.

Looked at in this way it would seem the culture determines the language, rather than the other way round. And surely to say we experience something but do not have the relevant language and therefore cannot express 'it' – a currently fashionable anxiety – is an error. Women, for example, need not worry that language is *incapable*, in a patriarchal society, of expressing their special feelings and ideas: it can be made to do so (as it has with, for instance, the introduction of the term *date rape*). The fault, where it exists, lies not with the language itself, but in an inability, for one reason or another, to combine imagination with the ready resources of the linguistic system (though of course, as chapters 6 and 7 recognize, even when language is created, chosen and uttered, it cannot guarantee itself a hearing).

In fact, Lakoff and Johnson call the making of metaphor an *imaginative rationality*, which is not, according to their thesis, a contradiction of terms. For seeing one thing in terms of another – the first step in making metaphor – involves imagination. But metaphors also require the reasoning of categorization, entailment and inference. The metaphorical understanding that time is money, for instance, entails that time is a limited resource, which in its turn entails that time is a valuable commodity (1980: 9). And users of the metaphor may therefore infer that time is to be treasured, not to be lightly spared, and certainly not to be frittered away. One thing leads, logically, to another.

But do metaphors, despite their 'imaginative rationality', always tell the truth? As we have said in the case of time, though we may speak of saving and spending it, it is not actually money, not really pounds and pence.

For their part, Lakoff and Johnson reject 'the objectivist view that there is absolute and unconditional truth', but they do so 'without adopting the subjectivist alternative of truth as obtainable only through the imagination, unconstrained by external circumstances' (1980: 193). Instead they see truth as relative – relative to our understanding of our experience. That is, metaphors are true for us in so far as our personal understanding of them matches our understanding of the experience they explain.

So, it *can* be true that time is like money – to be wisely spent, something too valuable to waste – if that is our experience. But it is equally possible that this formulation is, for someone else, an untruth. Young people who have never found paying jobs, for instance, might dispute its accuracy.

Still, supposing it is true for us: time is money. Even so, is this the whole truth and nothing but the truth? Or can metaphors be partial truths and, in consequence, have the potential to mislead?

Definitely: for metaphors work through 'a coherent network of entailments that highlight some features of reality and hide others' (Lakoff and Johnson 1980: 157). As they hide they may mislead. For, clearly, the 'match' between one thing (A) and its metaphorical comparison (B) cannot be perfect. If it were, these two would not be different, though comparable, entities. They would be one and the same thing. As it is, term A will not share all of B's features: term B will not have all of A's. For example, time (A) does not compare to money (B) in every single respect. We can see time being a limited resource, and therefore as having value, certainly. This is the aspect of money (something precious to be saved, spent, wasted) which the metaphor *Time is money* picks up and highlights. But time is not by any stretch of the imagination a hard currency. So time 'spent' – unlike pounds and pence – cannot be paid back if the 'goods' it buys are dud. Yet the fact you cannot get a refund on misspent time does not figure in our conventional use of the metaphor.

Looking at the metaphor the other way round, money (B) does not have all of time's (A's) possibilities. Money is not, for instance, the sort of thing one is usually quite relaxed about, enjoys playing with (unless it is Monopoly money) without anxiety. So if we accept the *Time is money* metaphor, and live preoccupied by its implications of prudence and hard work, we may not think much about the availability of *leisure* time. Or, if we do, we may, still remembering our habitual money metaphor, decide against investing in it: leisure may not 'yield' a sufficiently 'high return'.

This is precisely what is at issue for Lakoff and Johnson:

> not the truth or falsity of a metaphor but the perceptions and inferences that follow from it and the actions that are sanctioned by it.
>
> (1980: 158)

For there may be danger in what is hidden, risk in what is highlighted.

Perhaps this is why Salzman ends her poem railing against 'infernal time'. Time is not, for her poem's speaker, a 'well-made policy': rather, it is 'some black jester's dressed-up devastating game'. And this, to return to the beginning of this chapter, is the crucial point about linguistic determinism. Language is not something separate from human beings, driving them, deceiving them. On the contrary, language is part of ourselves and of our understanding. It is in human control, human determination. But, sometimes, it is taken over by some of its users, 'jesters' – to borrow Salzman's word – who may need to be unmasked.

Susan Sontag, in *AIDS and its Metaphors* (1990), and in her earlier discussion, *Illness as Metaphor* (1983), sets out to unmask the jester and expose the game.

METAPHORS WE LIVE – AND DIE – BY

It is the 'natural' but potentially damaging incompleteness of metaphorical understanding which lies behind the problem Susan Sontag identifies in her essay *AIDS and its Metaphors* (1990). That is, we may come upon metaphors which seem experientially accurate and so live by them. But, argues Sontag, their inevitable inadequacies, if not recognized, far from sustaining life, can kill.

In Sontag's view then, expressed in *AIDS and its Metaphors* and, with particular regard to cancer, in her earlier discussion *Illness as Metaphor* (1983), there are 'some metaphors we might well abstain from or try to retire' (1990: 5). But how can this be done if these metaphors appear 'true' in that their implications match their users' perceptions? Besides, as Lakoff and Johnson point out, though many metaphors have developed over a long period, others 'are imposed upon us by people in power – political leaders, religious leaders, business leaders, advertisers, the media, etc.' (1980: 159–60). How, if these powerful forces are 'jesters', can they be identified and their metaphors resisted?

The first step would be to scrutinize the metaphors, recognizing *all* their possible entailments, their hidden as well as their highlighted parts, checking to see if they, on careful reflection, do fit our own understanding of a situation sufficiently well to be accepted as true for us, whoever has introduced them to the language. Sontag's thought-provoking essay does precisely this for the metaphors of AIDS – as she understands them. The question is, do other hearers/users of these particular metaphors understand them in the same way? If they do, are they willing to refute and abandon them?

Sontag is particularly concerned with the metaphors of (a) staging, linked to the botanical image of a plant in full-bloom; (b) war and the military; (c) plague. She notes (d) the new metaphor of the sexual chain, and describes (e) her own economic metaphor of reactions to AIDS. All these are discussed in turn below.

Stages: full-blown

To begin with, Sontag is sceptical of the notion that AIDS has temporal *stages*. Infection with a human immunodeficiency virus (HIV) is, she maintains, recognized, labelled and seen as the first 'stage'. Then, when people 'show "early" and often intermittent symptoms of immunological deficit such as fevers, weight loss, fungal infections, and swollen lymph glands' they are said by some doctors to be suffering from 'AIDS-related complex' or 'ARC' (Sontag 1990: 21). Next, identified by the presence of some of a whole spectrum of illnesses, comes, so it is said, the third stage: acquired immune deficiency syndrome or AIDS.

Sontag argues that people are 'assigned' to ARC, the second 'stage'. Her choice of the word 'assigned' is significant, for she sees this – 'a kind of junior AIDS' – as purely a clinical construction which, presumably in Whorfian fashion, the language of those who recognize it supports and ratifies.

Overall she is critical of the linguistic formulation of stages because to speak of one 'stage' can imply that others will inevitably follow. To say that, at this stage, a person has HIV suggests that the next 'stage', ARC, will follow as night follows day, and that the development of AIDS is only a matter of time. In highlighting a relentless, fatal pattern, the image might inhibit the conception of other, less inevitable scenarios.

This pessimistic implication is particularly strong when the notion of staging is used in conjunction with the botanical metaphor *full-blown*: after the bud the full-blown flower; after full bloom, decay. Sontag explains her own objection, arguing in effect that the metaphor is not true because it does not match her understanding of the situation.

'Full-blown is the form in which the disease is inevitably fatal. As what is immature is destined to become mature, what buds to become full-blown (fledglings to become full-fledged) – the doctors' botanical or zoological metaphor makes development or evolution into AIDS the norm, the rule. I am not saying that the metaphor creates the clinical conception, but I am arguing that it does much more than just ratify it. It lends support to an interpretation of the clinical evidence which is far from proved or, yet, provable. It is simply too early to conclude, of a disease identified only seven years ago, that infection will always produce something to die from, or even that everybody who has what is defined as AIDS will die of it.

(1990: 28–9)

Jan Zita Grover takes the same view.

The only long-term prospective studies of people infected with HIV ... [suggest] that a sizeable proportion of them will develop the secondary infections and cancers that are termed AIDS. No data in the study, however, establish the inevitability of death from HIV infection.

(in Ricks and Michaels 1990: 147)

Moreover, Michael Callen describes himself as

a member of a small but persistent group of HIV heretics who cling to the belief that HIV ... has not been proven, by any acceptable standards of scientific inquiry, to be 'the cause' of AIDS. . . . There is a correlation with AIDS; but it used to be admitted in science that correlation was not the same thing as causation.

(in Ricks and Michaels 1990: 175)

Yet, as Callen says, he is a heretic in the minority. The implications of inexorable progress, highlighted by the metaphors of stages and of bud-to-bloom, are normally accepted, generally believed proven, and arguments to the contrary considered dangerous fantasy.

So perhaps, as a description of a process, there is truth in the metaphor of stages. Yet, being tested HIV positive, given our acceptance that it is likely to be followed by other stages of illness, can have immensely destructive psychological and practical consequences that affect relationships, jobs, finances – the list is endless. But would refusing to speak about stages alter the matter? Changing the language would not help if doing so merely avoided a reality. A better approach, at this point in our understanding of AIDS, would surely be to address the responses themselves, finding *more* language to express more perceptions about the actuality of AIDS, thereby encouraging greater understanding and compassion in reactions to those who are ill.

However, if stages is in some sense an accurate image, then the 'full-blown' concept may also represent a truth. Yet, if the idea of stages is accepted, it is a redundant term and, in any case, it is an insensitive, grotesque use of language which, I agree with Sontag, we would do well to 'retire', for, when using the adjective metaphorically in the context of AIDS, our minds must repress the irony of its usual link to flowers' richest, most attractive colours and perfumes.

War and the military

Sontag is also critical of the *war* and *military* metaphors used in connection with AIDS. War and disease have long been linked in language, sickness being seen as an invasion of the body which must defend itself. Sontag draws attention to the metaphysical poet John Donne's images of a canon of sickness battering the body and of fevers, like mines, blowing up the heart. In this century she notes the use of war metaphors in campaigns against tuberculosis. Italian 1920s posters imaged flies, carrying the disease, as enemy planes dropping bombs on the innocent. Others showed a figure of death, pinioned by swords, each of which had a label – sun, air, rest, hygiene – implying these may be used as 'weapons' in the 'fight' to 'combat' the 'attacker'.

However, the military metaphor has a Star Wars topicality in an application to AIDS which Sontag quotes from a *Time* magazine of late 1986:

> The invader is tiny. . . . Scouts of the body's immune system, large cells called macrophages, sense the presence of the diminutive foreigner and promptly alert the immune system. It begins to mobilize an array of cells that, among other things, produce antibodies to deal with the threat. Single-mindedly, the Aids virus ignores many of the blood cells in its path, evades the rapidly advancing defenders and homes in on the master coordinator of the immune system, a helper T cell. . . .On the surface of that cell, it finds a receptor into which one of its envelope proteins fits perfectly. . . . Docking with the cell, the virus penetrates the cell membrane.
>
> (Sontag 1990: 18)

Sontag objects to this kind of militarization of the disease, and of reactions to it, because she believes such language

> overmobilizes, it overdescribes, and it powerfully contributes to the excommunicating and stigmatizing of the ill. . . . We are not being invaded. The body is not a battlefield. The ill are neither unavoidable casualties nor the enemy. We – medicine, society – are not authorized to fight back by any means whatever.
>
> (Sontag 1990: 94–5)

Well, my dictionary defines casualties, on the one hand, as soldiers, wounded or killed, unavoidably, in battle. But certainly people with AIDS neither volunteered nor were conscripted for a war with the disease and the syndrome is avoidable, if with some difficulty. So, strictly speaking, the metaphor may be untrue: it does not match our experience.

Yet this same dictionary also suggests, for casualty, 'victim of a serious or fatal accident'. Is this not acceptable in regard to AIDS? It is unlikely that anyone deliberately sets out to be destroyed by AIDS. Is suffering from it not then a tragic accident?

In fact, however, Sontag objects to 'victim'. She writes, 'Victims suggest innocence. And innocence, by the inexorable logic that governs all relational terms, suggests guilt' (1990: 11). But whose guilt: the 'carrier', or the newly infected, or both? I take Grover's point (Ricks and Michaels 1990: 159) that using the phrase 'innocent victims' for some people with AIDS can imply that others with AIDS are less than innocent. For *innocent* should be a redundant term – given that a dictionary definition of a victim is something like 'one who suffers through no fault of his or her own'.

Calen too rejects *victim*, preferring the term 'people with AIDS', but his reasoning is different from Sontag's. He explains:

> To see oneself on screen and have the words AIDS victim magically flash underneath has a very different feel about it than when the description *person with AIDS* appears. Its very cumbersomeness is startling and makes the viewer ask: 'Person? Why person? Of course he's a person. . .' In that moment, we achieve a small but important victory. Viewers are forced to be conscious, if only for a moment, that we *are* people first.
>
> (Ricks and Michaels 1990: 177)

I am not certain, however, that the choice of 'person' would always have this positive effect. On the contrary, it seems to me so unspecific a word that the hearer does not have to consider the particular, individual *personality* with AIDS.

Nevertheless, there is another objection to the more usual 'victim'. Calen explains that the people with AIDS self-empowerment movement, founded in Denver, Colorado, resisted *victim* because it implies defeat, whilst in actuality those with AIDS are only from time to time passive and dependent on others. This seems to me an important objection but – again, personally – I am less sure about the National Association of People with Aids' dislike of the word. The Association objects to it on the grounds that to be a victim entails being victimized – and this, to the Association's way of thinking, may extend beyond the effects of disease itself to victimization through disrespect and the withholding of compassion. But would calling someone a victim really encourage people to victimize that person again, in other ways?

I doubt it. But of course, I have been emphasizing that I am arguing here purely from my personal responses to language as these fit – or do not fit – my personal experiences of its uses and contexts. Subjectivity of this kind is unavoidable and rational. For, to reiterate Lakoff and Johnson's argument, the point about the truth, or untruth, of metaphors and other uses of language is that the language is true, or not, in so far as it presently fits one's own understanding of it in relation to one's own life experience: to this extent it has an 'imaginative rationality'. The reader, then, may or may not respond to the metaphors of AIDS, or of anything else, precisely as I do.

As for Sontag, she is also critical if the battle metaphor entails people with AIDS as 'the enemy'. Her personal view would, surely, be shared by many. For it is a particularly objectionable use of language if, in the 'all's fair in love and war' tradition, it implies an enemy which may be fought by any means. Besides, the power of the concept is increased if those who are already seen, for other reasons, as the enemy can be imaged carrying the weapon of AIDS. Sontag writes:

> Authoritarian political ideologies have a vested interest in promoting fear, a sense of the imminence of takeover by aliens. . . . And AIDS is a gift to the present regime in South Africa, whose Foreign Minister declared recently, evoking the incidence of the illness among the mine workers imported from neighboring all-black countries: 'The terrorists are now coming to us with a weapon more terrible than Marxism: AIDS.'
>
> (1990: 61–2)

However, not everyone is unhappy with every use of the *war* and *enemy* metaphors. As Grover points out, a rejection of the notion that people with AIDS are themselves 'the enemy' does not preclude 'warring' against *structural* enemies, for example, legal discrimination, housing, employment. And mobilization against these 'enemies' and their 'weapons' is surely to be encouraged.

It is clear, then, that careful use of language is not a simple matter of marking words and structures as, once and for all, 'acceptable' or 'unacceptable': they only become so in each individual use and in relation one to another. The metaphor of 'stages', for instance, can, as suggested above, be less prejudicial where 'war' is declared against its unjust, social side-effects. (Besides, for some people who are ill it may be a relief to recognize a stage *mid-way* between initial infection and the development of AIDS itself, for the perception of ARC could offer respite, giving hope of an interval before the onset of very serious illness.[1]) Moreover, it is difficult to see anything hidden in the 'invaded' concept which is dangerous – when, that is, it refers to invasion by a virus and entails mobilization of the body's defences.[2]

However, for Sontag, metaphors of war blend with images of AIDS as *plague* – an invading enemy, as the notion has been traditionally understood, if ever there were one.

Plague

The word *plague*, used with reference to the syndrome of AIDS and the illnesses that attend it is not, if metaphor requires the yoking together of two quite distinctly different identities, strictly metaphorical. For plague is itself disease. But, metaphor or not, the concept has certain implications which can distort thinking about AIDS.

A dictionary definition of plague is 'very grave infectious disease', which would not seem inaccurate as a description of HIV and its role in the development of AIDS. But Sontag argues that plague is normally related to particular kinds of grave disease, 'the most feared diseases, those that are not simply fatal but transform the body into something alienating, like leprosy and syphilis and cholera' (1990: 45). And, if the body is alienating, so – leper-like – is the sufferer: alienating and alienated.

Moreover, explains Sontag, plagues imply 'the highest standard of collective calamity, evil, scourge . . . inflicted, not just endured' (1990: 44–5). They are typically understood to be inflicted as punishment, 'invariably regarded as judgments on society' (1990: 54) – moral judgements which make them fit, for many observers, their understanding of AIDS with its potential for sexual and drug-use transmission.

Further, to be one of these observers of AIDS is to be outside its sphere – and plague is conveniently assumed to come from elsewhere, from another sphere, another country, another community, another sort of person. These others, in the case of AIDS and this way of 'languaging' it, are deemed 'risk-groups', 'that neutral-sounding, bureaucratic category which also revives the archaic idea of a tainted community that illness has judged' (1990: 46).

And so two concepts, of war and of plague, fuse and complement. AIDS is, for those who accept such language as true, a warring enemy coming, like plague, from without and justly intent, like plague, upon attacking the guilty.

But there is another side to plague, another part of the AIDS picture 'illuminated' by the word. In Sontag's view the notion of plague, given its entailments of just deserts and highest collective calamity, fits comfortably with a peculiarly American dream: the notion of new beginnings for the righteous, fresh starts for the innocent, away from the contamination of destructive forces. For plague, as it is generally understood, sweeps away the 'undesirables' that it 'rightly' punishes, purging and cleansing as it goes.

Yet the incidence of AIDS has not only led to the take-over and adaptation of the old language of disease to this bigoted effect; it has triggered a new look at relationships, and an adjustment of language to express changed perceptions.

Chains of sex

Sex, Sontag points out, looks different nowadays. Its relationships are no longer couplings of the present, with the possibility of a future. Instead they may be seen as *chains*, connecting with a past and a future (1990: 72–3). The metaphor of the chain can of course be merely a benign set of links. Popular songs used to talk of 'chains of love', often welcoming their restraint. But here, in regard to AIDS, the metaphor recalls nothing but the fetters of a dreadful captivity. The language seems accurate thus far; but, like any metaphor, it has a number of less obvious entailments. Chains have to be chained: they need an 'actor'. Who, or what, imposes them – upon whom are they imposed – the innocent or the guilty?

Sontag also selects her own metaphors (based on consumer economy) which are connected with the 'chains' that can be seen between sex, society and AIDS.

From consumer boom to depression

Sontag writes:

> One set of messages of the society we live in is: Consume. Grow. Do what you want. Amuse yourselves ... risk-free sexuality is an inevitable reinvention of the culture of capitalism, and was guaranteed by medicine as well. The advent of AIDS seems to have changed all that, irrevocably.
>
> (1990: 76–7)

In consequence, she says – metaphorically –

> After two decades of sexual spending, of sexual speculation, of sexual inflation, we are in the early stages of a sexual depression.
>
> (1990: 76)

However, it is a depression which for some, she argues, is not entirely unwelcome. She observes that, alongside the self-indulgence of modern life, programmes of self-management and self-discipline have arisen and she suggests that responses to AIDS are of a piece with this movement.

> the response to AIDS is more than reactive, more than a fearful and therefore appropriate response to a very real danger. It also expresses a positive desire, the desire for stricter limits in the conduct of personal life. There is a broad tendency in our culture, an end-of-an-era feeling, that AIDS is reinforcing: an exhaustion, for many, of purely secular ideals – ideals that seemed to encourage libertinism or at least not provide any coherent inhibition against it – in which the response to AIDS finds its place.
>
> (1990: 78)

UNMASKING THE JESTER

It is apparent, then, that even if the metaphors of AIDS – the language of stages, blooms, war, plague and so on – are the sort of 'devastating game' that (in relation to 'time') Eva Salzman's poem describes playing on our perceptions, they can only do so with connivance. So they must. In order for words to become games, they must have players. And metaphors, as Lakoff and Johnson make clear, have to match their users'/players' understanding to some degree. This is their strength. But it is also their danger. For, as discussed earlier, metaphors are all, by definition, and of necessity, misfits. The difficulty lies, then, in identifying these deficiencies which, by their very nature, metaphors hide. Yet, although language can indeed be a seductive 'game', it is in our control to the extent that when a metaphor's entailments *dangerously* mismatch the totality of our present understanding, and the meanings we wish to convey, we can, if we will, expose and reject it in favour of a 'well-made policy'.

For example, it was pointed out to me (by Lindsay Davies, a Communications Studies student at The Nottingham Trent University) that British Sign Language, used by those who are deaf, originally chose for AIDS a sign which, in its imaging of a slow, crawling disease, was highly iconic. But activists within the deaf community encouraged a change to an abstract and therefore less emotive, more neutral, sign. Recently, however, this new sign has sometimes been corrupted, for it is possible to modify it to indicate transmission through anal sex and, thereby, to target particular groups. In consequence, in order to be as abstract as possible and avoid such complications, the letters A-I-D-S are now individually spelled out.

The same scrutiny can be applied to metaphors, in sign and spoken language, their usage modified if we wish to avoid some of their implications. However, Salzman hints at a reluctance to investigate and to alter language. In her poem, her acceptance of the notion of time – even though she finds it in some ways infernal – 'lets' her put off the plot and, presumably, take 'time out'. Moreover, when Sontag describes a certain metaphor as 'tenacious' (1990: 6), her own language (giving words 'physical' strength) is metaphorical; and it is perhaps mis-leadingly so, for it is surely the language user, not language itself, that tenaciously hangs on to partial truths. And it is not only those who originate a metaphor, but also those accepting and perpetuating its use, who play the jester and a jester's devastating game.

However, reluctance to let metaphors go is not surprising. Exposing the language game and unmasking its jesters (who may include ourselves) – abandoning metaphors which, on consideration of their full entailments, turn out to be grossly inaccurate and damaging – requires willingness, determination and sometimes courage. After all, jesters have traditionally been wise fools, and the nugget of truth that must always, by definition, reside for its user in a metaphor makes the retirement of destructive language, quite rightly called for by Sontag, easier to resist and far more difficult to achieve than the simple expurgation of words in a text.

Time out

Imagine there being no exacting word for time,
there being nothing to waste or save, invent
or slip away. Then who would fight the crime
of its fast passing? I'd take, say, the three-cigarette

train departing half-past-after-the-last-word
which wants saying (and not a moment too soon!)
while the numberless dial of my watch would refer
to a changing mise-en-scène winding from sun to moon,

or some event to an eventual end, when a black 'For Hire'
drives me home on its own good time. *Good* time. For tides
aren't for living by, but are only there to admire
occasionally on trips to the timeless seasides.

Nor do we milk cows, farm a natural time, say to friends:
'I'll meet you at the end of this cooking of rice'
or, more vaguely still: 'You know . . . when the afternoon ends.'
When? Would I be on time, guided by a smoky feel of night,
when it fell, in my bones – another made-up clocking-in machine?

But how would I measure these purposeful distances run,
or almost run, as the case would more likely seem?
The racers might just laugh or chat at the starting-gun.

Yet I wouldn't think to worry if I were late
for anything, wouldn't care by when which boat
came in. Stockbrokers would forget the date
and leisurely ask if you had the 'time' as a joke.

Some joke, infernal time! Not a word, not well-made policy,
but some black jester's dressed-up devastating game
which lets me put off the proverbial plot, infinitely,
so I could wait here forever before you finally came, or not.

SUGGESTIONS FOR FURTHER WORK

1 Identify the metaphors used in the first chapter of Susan Sontag's
Illness as Metaphor (1983) to talk about cancer and tuberculosis. Do
you think these metaphors are, particularly in the case of cancer, a part
of our everyday language? Do you feel they help to shape our thinking
about these illnesses? If so, do you think they shape it in a way
detrimental to our understanding and to those who are ill?

2 Could you suggest new metaphors which might improve our comprehension of illnesses including cancer and AIDS?

3
(a) Consider the everyday metaphor *Life is a journey*. Is this true for
you? If so, what does accepting the truth of this metaphor entail for
you? For me, for instance, it involves starting points, destinations,
roads of some kind. Does accepting the metaphor affect your
behaviour – that is, do you live by it?
(b) Are there any truths about your life and its 'journeying' that are
hidden if you accept this metaphor? Journeys probably need funding.
They can be held up by bad weather. Destinations are not always
what travellers hoped for. Had you thought of these implications? If
so, do you still feel, having reflected on these obscured implications,
that the metaphor is an acceptable way of thinking for you?
(c) Are there any other metaphors about life that you find as appropriate/
more appropriate?

4 Consider Shakespeare's metaphor, from *Macbeth*, 'Life is a tale told
by an idiot, full of sound and fury, signifying nothing.' What are its
implications? Does setting out to tell your *own* tale, your own 'life
story' (not necessarily that of an idiot!) shape your thoughts about the

events of your life in any particular way? If so, what, if any, are the consequences for your behaviour and attitudes? Think about what stories involve, like beginnings, middles and ends that are resolutions of some kind. Think about the roles people play in stories. Are you automatically the hero of your own life story? This exercise could be a helpful lead into chapter 5 and its discussion of personal narratives.

5   The narrative art of language

Poetry by Elizabeth Jennings and the short story 'Eveline' from James Joyce's *Dubliners*

This chapter looks at the shaping of perceptions through the work of the literary artist and also through the everyday craft of language, particularly in the structures of syntax and narrative. These structures are described on the lines of Labov's model of personal narratives (described in, for example, Labov and Waletsky, 'Narrative analysis: oral versions of personal experience' (1967) and with reference to models of language use explained by Halliday in Explorations in the Functions of Language *(1973) and by Greimas (as discussed by Toolan in* Narrative: a Critical Linguistic Introduction *(1988)). The heuristic and therapeutic value of story-telling is explored with reference to, for example, papers edited by Sarbin in* Narrative Psychology: the Storied Nature of Human Conduct *(1986).*

> . . . Death is another chapter.
> Now is only the poem.
> ('Let it be': Jennings 1989: 86)

Language itself is a theme running through many of Elizabeth Jennings' poems: for the artist, and for those who hear her, the shaping of words into sentences, poems and stories is, she writes, a craft, with mystical beginnings, and profound consequences.

A poem, she explains in 'Pigeons suddenly' (1989: 78), is not looked for but may be unexpectedly found, beginning and gathering force with the flourish, ease and natural grace of birds taking suddenly to the air. But, what the poem 'sings and tells and rhymes' is not the poet herself's own

> . . . plot
> Or life or worry. It is imagination
> Let loose and allowed to run wild.
> ('The luck of it' (1989: 79))

In consequence, poems can reveal new things: 'I write when the craft claims / What I never knew before' ('The arts' (1989: 23)). But their revelation is not exclusive to the poet:

> The poem is a way of making love
> Which all can share. Poets guide the lips, the hand.
> > ('The feel of things' (1989: 69))

And, because of this, the poet has a gift and a responsibility to care for others, especially in their fear. Jennings remembers her mother calming her childhood's terror. She had been 'afraid of a saint in a chapel / Of a huge cathedral because a white handerkerchief covered / His face' ('Some words of my mother's in childhood' (1989: 32)). That night she had cried and screamed in bed and her fear then

> . . . was an overmastering presence
> Larger than full moon or the tumbling clouds
> Or the blowing trees. Somebody strong had to speak
> And break the evil spell and so you did,
> My gentle mother.

The child and the fear may be still somewhere within the adult, but the poet's voice can be as the mother's: strong and calm enough to break the dark spell.

> Let me learn how to help those frightened others
> Who have no words but look to me for meaning
> Or who write and say they often read my poems,
> . . .
>
> > . . . Let those fraught figments
> In others' minds change to a rich peace
> When my poems arm them and take them over and soften
> However briefly the dreadful disturbance of life.

But I suggest this power is not confined to poetry. It is true that everyday language is unlikely to make the remarkable music of poetry, whose

> > . . . singing goes
> Up and up in swinging circles, in sound
> Where intimate conversation never goes.
> > ('Spring and a blackbird' (1989: 37))

Everyday language rarely has the smooth and steady cadence of poetry, the gentle and soothing rhythm that characterizes much of Jennings' art.

Nevertheless, day-to-day language may be a craft of significance. After all, we have heard that when the child was fearful it was not a poem but her mother's gently spoken words that broke 'the evil spell'. It was their 'pure . . . sentence / Which soothed the child', terrified by her memory of the saint.

> You said – and such magic there was of rich assurance
> In your quiet voice – 'He's laughing at you in Heaven'
> The room became small, the wind was friendly, the moon
> A face nodding with wise approval at me.
>   ('Some words of my mother's in childhood' (1989: 32))

The room, the wind, the moon and the image of the saint had not, of course, altered intrinsically. But the mother's words had given the child a new and comfortable way of seeing them. Her sentences were not untruths but fresh perceptions, 'hostile to shadows' like the poet's own song, which Jennings describes in 'Against the dark' (1989: 81) as

> Truthful, yes, obstinate too and yet
> Open to love that takes
> Language by the hand.

It is not surprising that 'ordinary' everyday talk can alter perspectives in this way, achieving a 'lift of language' ('Time for the elegy' (1989: 64)). For, carefully used, it has much in common with the making of art, the process and the outcome, that Jennings describes in 'The house of words' (1989: 74).

The house of words

> It is a house you visit but don't stay
> For long. Words leap from ledges. Verbs and nouns
> Ask for a sentence where they'll fit and say
>
> What you were unaware you thought. A dance
> Of meanings happens in your head. You start
> To learn a melody you half-heard once
>
> But can't remember wholly. Now verbs sort
> Themselves from nouns, and adjectives insist
> You use them with great care. There is a plot
>
> And a story where the parts of speech are placed
> By you and they will stay still only when
> You make their purpose clear. Now you are faced

With plot and characters. There's music in
Their lives and discourse. You must set them free
By knowing where facts stop and poems begin.

For there's a truth you find in artistry
Or it finds you. The lucky words appear
And now they have a theme and history.

But you must wait a little till you hear
The sound, the tune, the undertow of song,
And now you are made suddenly aware

Of music all these words find place among.
It swoops as birds do from the living air
And nests upon your house of words to throng

With messages you never hoped to hear
And greetings which sound best when they are sung.

                                        (1989: 74)

This ability, described here in 'The house of words' as knowing 'where facts stop and poems begin', is an art we can also recognize in our daily talk. For, though we may not speak in verse, we all practise the craft of language. In particular we are tellers of tales, narrators sorting – like the poet in a house of words – nouns and verbs, choosing adjectives, recounting our characters' history. And sometimes – because 'narration makes sense of the world' (Ratigan in Shepherd 1990: 170) – we, like the artist, discover messages we never hoped to hear, thoughts we did not know we had and, in life as in Jennings' poem, set our characters free.

THE SENSE OF NARRATIVE

Freud highlighted the power of narrative to order and explain life events. Polkinghorne concludes (1988: 121):

> Human beings are not simply constructions based on past events; they are also products of narrative structures. They exist in narrative creations and are powerfully affected by them.

Indeed, the psychologist, Theodore Sarbin, argues that 'Survival in a world of meanings is problematic without the talent to make up and to interpret stories about interweaving lives' (1986: 11). They are, he says, 'a guide to living' and 'a vehicle for understanding the conduct of others' (1986: x; see also Bruner 1986). Such tales are constantly told, by women and by men, in conversations over coffee, in the pub, on the phone, and also in the more formal settings of counselling and psychotherapy. As Elizabeth Jennings writes,

> . . . all
> We learn to care for are
> The quiet beginnings of the hint of a tale
> ('The start of a story' (1989: 80))

But what, precisely, are the linguistic components of a story? (For a development of the argument that follows see 'Healing narratives' in Shepherd 1990: 141–77.)

The form of everyday stories

Sentences are at the core of stories that occur in personal, everyday discourse, just as they are central to the artistic process defined in 'The house of words'. For (as also explained in chapter 1) their clauses, arranged in a particular order, form what the linguist, William Labov, has called a tale's *complication* (Labov and Waletsky 1967; Labov 1972; Labov and Fanshel 1977). Labov and Waletsky write (1967: 20–1):

> The basic narrative units that we wish to isolate are defined by the fact that they recapitulate experience in the same order as the original events.

These narrative units, or clauses, are thus the foundation of the tale – probably what Jennings refers to in her poem as 'plot' and 'facts' – for their temporal order cannot be changed without destroying the story or talking nonsense. For instance, the following arrangement of sentences is one story.

> Gertrude's husband, Hamlet's father, died. Gertrude, Hamlet's mother, and his Uncle Claudius married. Hamlet thought about murder.

Yet, re-arrange the same sentences and we have a different tale.

> Hamlet thought about murder. Then Gertrude's husband, Hamlet's father, died. Gertrude, Hamlet's mother, and his uncle married.

But (unless bigamy is involved) a further re-arrangement makes nonsense.

> Hamlet thought about murder. Gertrude, Hamlet's mother, and his Uncle Claudius married. Then Gertrude's husband, Hamlet's father, died.

Narrative clauses in the complication may be preceded, in the tales we tell each other, by a quick *abstract* of what is to come: 'Did I tell you about the time the Prince of Denmark wondered what to do about his Uncle Claudius?' It is a way of signalling that a story-teller is going to take the floor and needs an audience.

Then there is likely to be an *orientation*, setting the scene and naming its actors: 'It happened once upon a time at the court in Elsinore.'

Next comes the complication itself and, after it, there will probably be a *result*, what finally happened. In this case, 'Hamlet and his family died and there was a new king.'

Then, in personal narratives, occurring in conversation, there may be a *coda*: a signal that the story is over and other people may now have the floor: 'So that was that. Now tell me what *you* did yesterday.'

But, as they stand, these components only add up to what Rothery and Martin (1980) call a 'recount', the sort of thing heard regularly from young children and also from ourselves when offering, say, a bland chronicle of our day.

> I went to the bank and cashed that cheque, then booked the theatre tickets and paid for the papers on my way home.

This story-teller has recounted 'theme and history' as they are described in 'The house of words' – but not, I suggest, what Jennings may mean by the 'truth'. That comes, in Labovian terms, in the *evaluation*, which finds the point of the tale, explains what it is all about, reveals the truth of the matter as the narrator sees it.

Evaluation can appear right at the end of the complication in the form of an overt and clear-cut comment. The clauses recounting the day's events are evaluated in this way in the following version's additional sentence:

> I went to the bank and cashed that cheque, then booked the theatre tickets and paid for the papers on my way home. *It's amazing – all that money gone between the bank and here!*

A closing comment on *Hamlet* might be:

> It all goes to show – family relationships are delicate and dangerous things. Disturb them at your peril!

However, evaluation can take place at any point in a tale and be signalled in any and every choice of word, sound and grammar. Hamlet, with his dying breath, urges Horatio to 'tell my story' (V.ii.331) and, as Fortinbras contemplates the bodies littering the castle hall, Horatio promises he will indeed explain 'How these thing came about'

(V.ii.362). He begins by giving a rapid abstract of the narrative to come – an abstract that also evaluates the events he is going to recount: they were, in his estimation, 'carnal, bloody, and unnatural' (V.ii.363). These choices of judgemental adjectives (Jennings did say that 'adjectives insist / You use them with great care'!) epitomize the way Horatio perceives all that has happened. They explain the truth as he personally sees and evaluates it: the hasty marriage of Gertrude and Claudius was, in his view, 'unnatural' and the root of the tragedy.

But evaluative truth is relative. Laura Bohannan told Hamlet's story to village elders in the African bush and to them Gertrude and Claudius' behaviour was by no means unnatural. For, from this particular African perspective, Claudius did the honourable thing in marrying his brother's widow so promptly. So 'it is clear', the listeners said to Bohannan, 'that the elders of your country have never told you what the story really means' (in Morris 1956: 186).

Different people, that is, see and evaluate what a story 'really' means from their different points of view. (Indeed, the subjectivity of perception may itself be one of the central themes of *Hamlet*.) Moreover, the same person may also see a different point at different times. Robinson and Hawpe find that story-tellers practise 'narrative repair', a potentially unending process of reassessing a basic plot, for 'interpretive perspectives change prompting reevaluation of . . . the original account' (Sarbin 1986: 123).

The essential narrative clauses then, those sentences that give the story its immutable facts – its plot, as it were – remain constant. But the way these are understood is personal, flexible and expressed in the evaluative language choices, of word and sound and syntax, in which we express the clauses of the tale.

> . . . the parts of speech are placed
> By you and they will stay still only when
> You make their purpose clear.

Choosing parts of speech

The concept of language choice has run through several chapters so far. Language users are essentially creative, not needing to parrot sentences they have heard before but theoretically making free selection from the options available in the phonological, lexical and syntactic 'systems' of their particular language. And, in everyday language as well as in the poetry of 'The house of words', 'verbs sort / Themselves from nouns' asking 'for a sentence where they'll fit'. The sentences themselves 'fit' in narratives when we have chosen and arranged them in a way that, for us, makes sense of – 'truthfully' evaluates that is – the way we see things.

In school, verbs used to be called 'doing words' and, if approximate, it is not a bad definition of their function. It explains their central role in stories. For example, in effect, Sutton-Smith's analysis (in Sarbin 1986: 83–8) of narratives told by western children deals with the *verb phrases* of narratives. For he finds their plots tend to adapt through four stages, each, in a progressive pattern of 'doing', representing a gradually increasing sense of ability to overcome difficulties. The first level of story-telling centres on the 'doings' of conflict: maybe a monster threatens. The second concentrates on evasion: escape from the monster. The third includes restraint: the monster captured. The fourth achieves transformation: the monster is rendered powerless for all time. Sutton-Smith finds that fourth-level plots 'approximate to the hero myths of the western world within which heroes and heroines brought under duress, undertake tasks which resolve their problems' (Sarbin 1986: 89).[1]

Yet the resolution of difficulty is not confined to the doings of folk and fairy tale but is also a focus of everyday stories that turn mere 'recounts' of events in temporal order into something problem solving and heuristic. And 'events', of course, and their difficulties, may include those of thinking, feeling, saying, as well as physical activity.

But, naturally, verbs do not, on their own, make events. To be complete they need nouns (and pronouns), the class of words that labels participants (not always people, of course) involved in the doing. Here Greimas's narrative model of six *actants* (1966) is helpful, for these actants (three interrelated pairs) may be said to approximate to the *noun phrases* of the sentences that make up narratives. The actants are (as explained in Toolan 1988: 93–5):

superhelper–giver/receiver–beneficiary
subject/object
helper/opponent

These categories apply particularly neatly to folk-tale fiction. For example, the subject, Cinderella, achieves her object, the Prince, partly through her helper, the glass slipper, despite her opponents, the Ugly Sisters. In all of this she is the beneficiary of assistance from her superhelper, her Fairy Godmother. However, these same roles can also (as discussed below) be identified in modern fiction. Moreover, they are found yoked to the verbs of everyday, personal narration where our classification and assessment of roles is a crucial part of our evaluation of life events. Do we see – evaluate – this person, or that, as helper or opponent in the doings of our story? Moreover, do we, in the process of Robinson and Hawpe's 'narrative repair' (referred to above, p. 85), alter our assessment?

The uniting of verbs and nouns, in these perceptually important ways, may happen through choices from the *transitivity* system. This was discussed, along the lines of Halliday's systemic grammar (a description of which may be found in Halliday 1973), in chapter 1.

We have the option of choosing English verbs that are transitive or intransitive, or have the potential to be either. The transitivity system can express *processes*. These may be 'physical' – to walk, to run, to create; or they may be 'mental' – to think, to decide, to fear. Verbs behaving transitively can take an object (in the syntactic sense): *The handler walked the dog*. When behaving intransitively they do not: *The dog walked*. There are thus 'participants' (the type we are concerned with here will usually be nouns or pronouns) in the verbs. Halliday describes their *roles* in relation to the verb as agent, patient, beneficiary and so on. When the verb is transitive its agent, its 'doer' if you like, acts upon patient, beneficiary or whatever: *the handler* (agent) *walked the dog* (patient). Participants in intransitive verbs, however, keep themselves, as it were, to themselves. But, whether the verb is transitive or intransitive, there is always an 'affected' participant. The agent and the affected are different in verbs that are transitive, but are one and the same when they are intransitive. Passive constructions, unlike active ones, can of course omit reference to their agents. We can say *The dog was walked by the handler* but could choose instead to miss out the 'actor' and simply say *The dog was walked*.

The agent in a sentence of the transitivity system might, in Greimas's actant sense, appear as a story's subject (**Cinderella** *lost her slipper*), or object (**Prince Charming** *found it*), or opponents (*The* **Ugly Sisters** *tried it on*) and so on. Equally, Greimas's subject, and so on, could be patient: *The Ugly Sisters hated* **Cinderella**. The two language models, that of Halliday's transitivity and Greimas's actants, describe sentences and narratives in different but complementary ways.

It will be remembered, from chapter 1, that Lok (a subject actant of the story *The Inheritors*) selected options from the transitivity system but, tragically, was unable to do so in constructive ways. The distinction made by Crites (Sarbin 1980: 160), between sense and experience, was noted here. Lok sensed things that happened to him and around him, but he could only 'experience' fully those events to which he gave the judging, evaluative shape of language. And he could only deal effectively with those he 'languaged' in ways that matched – and thus made manageable for him – his changing reality. As it was, Lok's inability to recognize the inheriting tribe's powerful and hostile agency contributed to his demise. The same may be said of ourselves: much that we encounter remains formless and beyond our controlling agency until we put it into words that organize, clarify and evaluate in realistic ways. Our selections of nouns and verbs, participants and their doings, from the transitivity system are important evaluative choices.

They are selections which are of course affected by our choices of other parts of speech, including adverbs and adjectives. It was noted earlier that Horatio chose adjectives which described the activities of Hamlet's family as 'unnatural' – but other witnesses, told of these same doings, did not.

It can be said, then, that in a sense we 'see through syntax', perceiving the events of our lives and the participants in them through linguistic choices which organize and evaluate them. What follows looks first at the language choices of fiction before turning to the narratives of real life.

Seeing through syntax

Actants

Toolan (1988: 95–6) relates Greimas's *actants* to fiction through James Joyce's short story, 'Eveline' (from *The Dubliners*, first published 1914: Joyce 1977: 40–4). Here, the *subject*, in Greimas's sense, is Eveline herself. Her *object*, to begin with anyway, is the happiness she sees in freedom from her *opponent*, her father and his restrictions and abuse. Frank, in giving her a chance to leave her family home, seems to be the *helper* she needs in securing her object. But will Eveline, utimately, be the *receiver* of her desires? Will she, that is, overcome her difficulties? The answer is not as straightforward as it might be in those children's stories where monsters are defeated and in fairy-tales where the princess gets her prince and lives happily ever after. For Eveline's story becomes more complex, her object, as Toolan points out, altering as she comes near to achieving it when, after all, she sees good in her father and also remembers she had promised her mother to keep the home together for as long as possible. So Frank, starting out as Eveline's helper, in a sense ends – in her estimation – as her opponent, his behaviour confusing her in her attempt to clarify and secure her objectives.

But Greimas identifies a further 'actant': a giver or *superhelper*. And Eveline may seem to look for such a giver when she prays to God to give her direction – to show her her 'duty'. Yet this is not a simple, direct appeal. Fairy-tale subjects know what they want, make their three wishes, and fairy godmothers, in one guise or another, simply grant them with their magic wands. But Eveline is neither so single-minded nor so dependent. As Toolan points out, she asks for help *to help herself* – to look within herself and find her own answers. Moreover, Toolan believes that in modern story-telling generally 'the role of higher help, outside certain varieties of science fiction . . . and comic strips of the Superman variety, seems to be becoming attenuated' (1988: 94).

Yet does Eveline find an answer – does she really look for resolution? Toolan suggests that some readers will see Eveline's turning her back on Frank as a clear and independent choice or, at least, personally made with God's support. However, he points out that Joyce goes on to describe her as '"passive, like a helpless animal", which hardly fits an interpretation of Eveline as powerful arbiter' (1988: 96). Indeed, it is as if the life had gone out of her. For in the closing words of the story, Eveline's eyes gave Frank 'no sign of love or farewell or recognition' and it seems to me that no help has been received, no object – of any sort – achieved. But then, throughout her story Eveline has appeared relatively passive. Choices from the transitivity system suggest this from the narrative's first sentences.

Transitivity

These syntactic choices sometimes appear to be those of the narrating voice, describing Eveline's story as he sees it. But frequently the style seems to be that of 'free indirect speech', fusing narrator and character viewpoint. For example, the first and third sentences in the following extract seem to come from the narrating voice. The second and fourth sound as if they stem from Eveline's own thoughts.

> She had consented to go away, to leave her home. Was that wise? She tried to weigh each side of the question. In her home anyway she had shelter and food; she had those whom she had known all her life about her.

We are getting Joyce's narrator's description of Eveline's story, then, but we are also privy to the way she herself saw and evaluated matters. And, on the whole, in terms of transitivity, Eveline seems to have cast herself as victim or patient.

In her story's very first sentences she merely sits and is tired. She seems hardly to control her own body. Her 'head' – not 'she' – is affected participant in a structure that acknowledges no other agency but itself in the arrangement of her posture: 'Her head was leaned against the window curtains.' And she does not actively seek and register her sensations. They are merely there: 'in her nostrils was the odour of dusty cretonne'. At this point, the evening appears to be the only active, affecting, agent: she watched it 'invade the avenue'. The choice of verb 'invade' – an odd word, with its sense of conquering, even violating power, to describe a change of light and atmosphere – emphasizes Eveline's contrasting inertia and weakness.

And nothing much changes as the story develops. Eveline's active agency, as she recalls it, is confined to dusting, and shopping, and serving – for other people. In the relationship with Frank, he is the active agent, she the affected participant: he took her to the theatre, teased her, confused her pleasantly with his singing, told her of his exciting life. It is true that, after his quarrel with her father, Eveline did take action and meet her lover, but she did so secretly. And though she actively 'consented' to go away with Frank, she is at once doubtful and fretful.

Activity, self-assertive activity, resides for Eveline only in an imagined future: 'she was about to explore'. And even this future would be in Frank's gift, not in Eveline's autonomous choice and control: he, she believed for a time at least, 'would save her . . . give her life . . . take her in his arms . . . save her'. Yet, when he calls her to him for the last time, she answers nothing, does nothing, cannot even consent to be his 'patient' and be 'saved'. She can only cry out in an anguish of confusion.

She had tried, earlier, to make some rational decision, to see and evaluate her life story clearly and take charge of it: 'She tried to weigh each side of the question.' But her weighing and balancing was not even-handed, for the best of her memories came to the fore and did so without challenge, clouding the issue, tormenting her with conflict, so that 'now . . . she was about to leave it she did not find it a wholly undesirable life'.

However, a more thorough, more probing evaluation of her story would have noted that, in these relatively happy parts of her recollection, Eveline was a child: her mother was alive, the family had picnicked at the Hill of Howth and her father had put on her mother's bonnet and made Eveline and her brothers laugh. Or, she was older but *as* a child, ill and, for once, protected by her father. That is, in the few moments Eveline recognizes as best, she was acting as patient, beneficiary or some such role to her parent's stronger agency. It is perhaps no wonder, therefore, that she seems to have seen Frank too in the light of a carer, a kind of father maybe, and not as a sexual and equal partner. Whilst he might 'perhaps', she thought, give her love, he would certainly 'fold' her in his arms (and the choice of verb here suggests protection not passion) and so save her. Her lack of confidence, and her limited experience of safety and warmth, leave Eveline a child in relation to Frank.

True, she appears to have envisaged an adult role for herself in the future: 'she would be married' and therefore treated 'with respect'. But here she is only describing a state, of marriage, and other people's behaviour – their agency – towards her. She has no image of a new Eveline whose life will *actively command* such respect.

And, in any case, did she really believe she would be respected? She certainly imagines no respect from her acquaintances at the Store. If she were to 'run away with a fellow', perhaps they would say 'she was a fool'.

This passage seems to be written in the free indirect speech which echoes Eveline's own words. And, in describing her notion of other people's opinions it hints at her own estimate of her self. The words are therefore Eveline's own evaluation of her *projected* story line. (It will be recalled that in chapter 1 the place of narrative form in future planning was mentioned: we can 'language' and evaluate the future, as well as the past, in the form of stories shaped around participant roles and processes.) Her comments reflect her minimal self-confidence. But it is possible they also signal some insight into her relationship with Frank, for it would, very likely, be a foolish thing to go away with him as a dependent child.

Yet insight does not develop any further to evaluate Eveline's past story and to guide her future actions. In the first sentence of the narrative her senses were, as we saw, quite deadened. They seem to wake a little later, but only to register more consciously the pull of the known and the certain. Eveline is now, deliberately, 'inhaling' the odour of the dusty curtain (it is not just 'there', in her nostrils). And she is hearing the organ music that reminds her of her mother and of a daughter's responsibility. But it is probably not so 'strange', as Eveline thinks, that the nostalgic air 'should come' this very night. It is more likely (in Crites' sense) that it has been played and sensed before, but this time, inclining to the security of the familiar, Eveline is choosing to acknowledge and experience it. It is ironic that, through this tiny act of will, she reinforces, in terms of transitivity and life, her role as 'patient', for 'the very quick of her being' is overcome by the spell of memory and duty.

But could Eveline, in her circumstances in Catholic Dublin at the beginning of the twentieth century, have behaved any differently, been any less passive and accepting? The facts of her existence – a daughter's responsibility, a father's violence, a religion's orthodoxies and a community's prejudices (her story's essential narrative clauses, as it were) – could not be changed easily, if at all. Hers is a story that seems, almost inevitably, to involve sacrifice.

However, if she had to remain with her father and her job in the Store, Eveline might at least have combated her depression through the relative autonomy of seeing these elements of her life clear-sightedly – not reducing her perception of her role to that of a fool, or distorting it to child of a 'reliable' and 'loving' parent, or to child in need of and grateful for paternal attention.

Perhaps if, when she was weighing and balancing the scales of her life, Eveline had had someone to talk with, she might have been able to practise the kind of 'narrative repair' described by Robinson and Hawpe. If so, her perceptions might then have been clearer and more in her autonomous control. She might then have seen and 'languaged' that last moment at the docks quite differently. Instead of believing Frank 'would drown her' she might have wondered if she – not the sailor – was the agent drawing her metaphorically down into the water, her actions those of self-destructive resistance.

As it is, her favourite brother is dead and the other, Harry, is nearly always away. Nor, it would seem, had Eveline friends to consult with and support her, only acquaintances and her employer at the Store. And so, in the event, her life will probably be as her mother's before her, one of 'commonplace sacrifices': not willing and worthwhile sacrifice, but *commonplace* sacrifice, borne not chosen. The particular nature of the cultural, social and personal pressures that Eveline endured, have blurred her vision and overwhelmed her sense of self and her access to autonomy, so that narrative repair is impossible and she is overwhelmed in 'final craziness'.

In any case, speculation about possible alternatives is fruitless, since the fictional Eveline's story remains for all time suspended at the moment of her separation from Frank. It is more profitable to consider how the 'narrative repair' of real-life stories might be supported.

The 'lift of language'

As with Jennings' poetry, a story's 'parts of speech are placed / By you', the teller of the tale. But we frequently tell and retell our stories. We cannot change their basic plots: we cannot tamper with their essential narrative clauses. But we can re-evaluate them, rethinking, for example, the roles of participants in the processes of our stories, until our narratives perceive the truth of our tales in ways with which we can live.

However, Jennings writes

. . . It would be
Unjust if grief could be written
Out in a facile charge . . .

. . . Words are not sunlight
After the dark night or terrible tempest of grief.
If they were it would not be right.

('Justice' (1989: 120))

She is surely correct. Talking once of narrative re-evaluation to doctors and psychiatrists who had dealt with the injured minds of survivors from rail and air disasters, I felt naive to suggest that words could 'repair' narratives and lives in the way I have in mind. And yet, perhaps they can – but not in the days and weeks during and soon after distress and tragedy. Perhaps the creative energy of 'everyday' language becomes effective, more than a 'facile charge', only later. I am turning once again to Jennings to borrow an explanation:

The lift of language is an art one earns

After the dumb guilt and hidden suffering.
So now my memory is a room as clean
As any broom can sweep, and I can fling

The windows wide upon a Winter scene
About to alter. Blackbirds rise and sing
And snowdrops mean defiance that has been

Gathering in the quiet Winter.

('Time for the elegy' (1989: 64))

The lift of language may come in the informal contexts of self-reflection or conversation with friends, or in the formal settings of therapy.

Careful listening

We constantly tell stories, to friends and acquaintances; and friends may encourage a tale's re-evaluation, questioning our point of view. But this frequently involves the listener's own, alternative perception – and the listener does not have to live our life story! The professional counsellor, on the other hand, is perhaps a modern-day version of Greimas's 'superhelper' – not dictating a new story but listening carefully in ways which help the client towards narrative discovery.

This more detached listening is offered by supportive organizations like the Samaritans. I am grateful to its volunteers, particularly those at the Peterborough Branch, for welcoming my interest in their work and for giving me their very helpful assistance.

Samaritans

Samaritans choose their own language, particularly its grammar, carefully. An image used in their training explains why. Callers, people in distress, are imagined as if they were trapped in a dark pit. The Samaritan, listening to them, is looking over its edge.

Now, the listener could put a metaphorical ladder down into the pit's depths, and call out instructions for getting on to it and out – for extracting themselves from their old story, as it were. But instructions, syntactic *commands* – to do this, be that – are really not viable because, from a secure and detached vantage point at the pit edge, no outsider can fully understand life down in its darkness.

Therefore, the Samaritan also resists making *statements* about that darkness. No one can comment with perfect authority on a life story in which they have not been a participant.

However, the Samaritan listener can offer acceptance and comfort – by trying to share the darkness of the pit. That can only be done through understanding. And understanding may be achieved by asking *questions*, open questions that leave room for more than a yes/no answer and so give a caller a chance, if s/he wants to take it, of telling his/her story. Here is the time and space, provided by someone who, not being a participant in the tale, can listen with care but without pressure – an opportunity for the caller to re-evaluate his/her story's plot and to find a new perception of the darkness, a fresh understanding which might provide a way out of the pit.

Nevertheless, Samaritans are prepared to accept that there may be no escape route: as they listen, the story's evaluation may remain the same, its narrator seeing no possible scope for change to a more bearable perception. But still, through their willingness to listen, Samaritans *accept* that unchanging evaluation and so offer the comfort that the fictional Eveline was unable to find. The caller telling his/her story is valued: none is the unimportant fool that Eveline thought herself.

The story-teller is, of course, equally valued by any supportive agency. Some approaches, however, like psychodynamic therapy, whilst accepting the narrative a person brings to counselling, set out to encourage its re-evaluation.

Psychodynamic therapy

I am grateful to psychotherapist Bernard Ratigan for discussing with me his own psychodynamic work, carried out in student counselling and in the Health Service. His view of story-telling, described briefly below, is recorded in full in Shepherd 1990: 167–75.

Ratigan confirms the constant use of story-telling and of narrative repair in counselling and therapy. In fact, he believes that if stories are not present

> this may be a signal of continuing inner chaos. Disintegration of language can signal disintegration of the internal world. Disintegration can be at the level of syntax. But it can also disrupt the narrative form.
>
> (Shepherd 1990: 170)

Over a number of sessions with him, he explains, people's stories do alter: their narrators seem, he suggests, to be 'nudging on a ratchet towards something which is disclosing about themselves' (Shepherd 1990: 171).

Unlike a call to Samaritans, however, there is a time limit on this story-telling. Each session lasts fifty minutes and it would seem that the pressure of such a boundary helps to get 'an autonomous part of the patient moving', encouraging talk and constructive narration (Shepherd 1990: 168). In fact, helping the patient to find autonomy – something that James Joyce's Eveline never achieved – is one of a therapist's prime goals. (This may seem at odds with Bernard Ratigan's own choice of the word 'patient', given its implications of passiveness, but he prefers *patient* because he feels the alternative, *client*, takes no account of the intensive work and, indeed, suffering that may be involved in therapy.) Ratigan's own language is therefore designed to offer those who come to him 'ownership, ownership of actions and feelings' and of their own stories (Shepherd 1990: 169).

However, he himself actually says very little. After all, it is the patient's story which is important, not the therapist's. So, most of the time, only minimal responses – *I see*, *yes*, *go on* – are given, brief encouragements which can give the story-teller the confidence and reassurance to continue.

But, occasionally, *alternative* language may be offered: *It sounds to me as if you might be saying. . .* Sometimes, proffered alternatives relate to the roles and processes of transitivity, inviting those seeking help to alter their noun or verb phrases in ways that encourage a new way of 'seeing through syntax'. If, for instance, a narrator says, *You feel bad when that happens*, or even, *One feels bad when that happens*, the alternative, *I feel bad when that happens*, might be suggested. This small pronominal change can help the speaker recognize ownership of a feeling – and, with the recognition of ownership may come a sense of control and the ability to accept or to change.

A clear-sighted ownership of actions can also be encouraged. If someone says, *I couldn't do that*, Ratigan might, so long as the rest of the patient's story seems to allow the change, offer instead (altering modal verbs), *I **didn't** do that*, or even *I **wouldn't** do that*. Someone who has entered the session convinced of a personal inability might then, seeing themselves through new language, begin to consider the possibility that s/he had *chosen* not to do a certain thing: inability was not the cause of inaction.

Any new language which may be suggested is not offered as an absolute, but as an 'irritant' to the client's own fresh thinking – his/her fresh storying, as it were. Ratigan explains:

> The people using it are encouraged to see themselves not as victims but as actors. They can choose to recognize themselves as responsible. And they are then at liberty to expand that responsibility.
>
> (Shepherd 1990: 169)

They are at liberty to expand and tell their stories as they choose.

And so, in therapy, personal narratives come to be told and retold, evaluated and re-evaluated. But is there an end story, one authentic tale from which we move no further? Ratigan agrees that a story's basic 'plot' would have an immutable authenticity. If a person has lost a loved one, or has been divorced, or raped, these are the tale's essential 'narrative clauses'. But, he believes, there is no ultimate story, only *approximations* derived from different evaluations. And re-evaluation, he explains,

> is always a provisional understanding . . . it gets more valuable, not more valid precisely. It is a question of readiness. Later readings might have been too difficult to face earlier. . . . My therapeutic task is to offer patients their story in a tolerable way. If it is too powerful at the time it can destroy the world they have got going for them. Or if they aren't ready it will bounce off them. The patient is really doing the work and . . . will go over the same story repeatedly until the new story has arrived; that is, when the perspective on the old story has changed.
>
> (Shepherd 1990: 171–2)

In fact, a moment's thought confirms that all of us go over and over our stories constantly, adjusting our understanding of them, sometimes in professional counselling sessions but most often privately, in our heads, or in conversation with friends and family. Narratives tell the stories of our lives. Yet, more than this, they can, as Bernard Ratigan's comments appear to confirm, be *givers* of life, re-evaluations which permit new perceptions, new ways of seeing that allow us to take increased control of our day-to-day existence.

Through narration we can discover, like Elizabeth Jennings in her poetry, the messages we never hoped to hear.

SUGGESTIONS FOR FURTHER WORK

1 'Clay' is another story from James Joyce's *Dubliners* (1977: 83–8). It includes sentences which come directly from a narrating voice, some which report Maria's thoughts indirectly through the narrator, and some – as in 'Eveline' – which are apparently in free indirect speech. Together these sentences make up, in Labov's sense, the tale's complication and its evaluations. Do the evaluations of all three 'voices' present the same understanding of the story? I suggest they do not: Maria and the narrating voice may view her experiences rather differently. Maria – like clay itself? – seems to me to mould her comprehension of her life's events and its relationships to fit her very understandable desire to be loved and appreciated. First, for example, she is satisfied with her lot at the launderette. Then she is happy to be the Maria she thinks Joe and his family want. But I feel the narrating voice sometimes interprets the people surrounding Maria differently than she does. Moreover, these people do not always see things quite as Maria does. Do you also identify aspects of language which carry these alternatives ways of seeing?

2 Different newspapers often report the same story from different perspectives with different audiences in mind. Take two papers published on the same day and look at their treatment of a particular event. Do they offer significantly different impressions of the participants and processes involved? If so, identify these and describe them with the help of Greimas's model of actants and/or Halliday's model of transitivity.

3 Record (with their participants' permission) some conversations. Do they include personal narratives of the kind described by Labov? If so, clearly identify the portion of talk which equates with an 'abstract', a 'complication' and so on. Which aspects of the language seem to be 'evaluations'?

4 Try writing down a part of your own life story. Better still, look back at an old diary. Is there, on reflection, any room for narrative repair here? Could you, that is, take a fresh look at your story's language and reword it in ways which, though still truthful, are, on reflection, more helpful, more constructive ways of seeing things? If language changes are possible, what would they be? Do they involve choices from the transitivity system or other aspects of syntax, selections of adjectives, alterations to other vocabulary? If so, why?

6 Standard and Non-standard English

The Dorset poetry of William Barnes, with reference to Tennyson's Lincolnshire monologues and Tom Leonard's Glasgow poem

This chapter rejects negative attitudes to Non-standard language and, with some reference to current developments in English teaching, and to nineteenth- and twentieth-century poetry, stresses its psychological, cultural and expressive value.

The vaïces that be gone

When evenen sheädes o' trees do hide
A body by the hedge's zide,
An' twitt'ren birds, wi' plaÿsome flight,
Do vlee to roost at comen night,
Then I do saunter out o' zight
   In orcha'd, where the pleäce woonce rung
   Wi' laughs a-laugh'd an' zongs a-zung
     By vaïces that be gone.

There's still the tree that bore our swing,
An' others where the birds did zing;
But long-leav'd docks do overgrow
The groun' we trampled beäre below,
Wi' merry skippens to an' fro
   Bezide the banks, where Jim did zit
   A-plaÿen o' the clarinit
     To vaïces that be gone.

How mother, when we us'd to stun
Her head wi' all our naïsy fun,
Did wish us all a-gone vrom home:
An' now that zome be dead, an' zome
A-gone, an' all the pleäce is dum',
   How she do wish, wi' useless tears,
   To have ageän about her ears
     The väices that be gone.

Vor all the maïdens an' the bwoys
But I, be marri'd off all woys,
Or dead an' gone; but I do bide
At hwome, alwone, at mother's zide,
An' often, at the evenen-tide,
   I still do saunter out, wi' tears,
   Down drough the orcha'd, where my ears
   Do miss the vaïces gone.

William Barnes

(Jones 1962: 204; all subsequent page references for Barnes' poems
are to this edition)

SING AGAIN TOGETHER

The language, people and poetry of Dorset were the mainsprings of
William Barnes' nineteenth-century life. Born in 1801, on a small-
holding in the Blackmore Vale, he grew to love the land, appreciate its
labouring families and speak their dialect. But he augmented his
elementary schooling with voracious reading and, after a spell as a
solicitor's clerk, he became a schoolmaster, a clergyman and a
polymath: he was an accomplished musician, artist, scientist, journal-
ist and internationally known linguist. He was also a poet, writing
about Dorset in the Vale of Blackmore dialect and sometimes in
Standard English.

His roles as a parson and a teacher fused with his talent as a writer
and his knowledge as a linguist. Writing poetry was, in Barnes' view,
a means of 'Steering and guiding the soul to setting forth the good and
the loveworthy that men's minds would more readily take and hold it'
(Levy 1960: 17). To this end he wanted to 'light up [rustic life's] more
lovely features' (1841: 510). In consequence his poetry contains, as
H.J. Massingham remarked (1942: 408), 'all the graciousness and
greeness and floweriness of the Dorset pastures'. These are evident in
the clear and colourful images of the poems, the sun-burned workfolk
in their snow-white sleeves, the hedgerows' scarlet poppies and
yellow cowslips, their blackberries and dewy spiders' webs, the
maidens 'sheening hair' and rosy blush, the sky-blue shells of
thrushes' eggs. They are here in the ploughing and the hay-making, the
reels and the jigs, the fairs and the harvest suppers. They are here in the
sounds of laughter and sing-songs, in the noise of gently 'huffling'

wind and of frozen grass crunching under foot – and in the music of
church bells, pealing out 'vor all the naïghbours round', those loving
friends and families who are at the heart of Barnes' work ('Lydlinch
bells', 302). Above all, rural Dorset is manifest in Barnes' use of the
regional variety of English which he prized, both as a local man and as
a linguist.

John Barrell has found all this 'too hopelessly nostalgic to be at all
serviceable' (Barrell and Bull 1982: 431). But I shall be suggesting that
Barnes' poetry is, on the contrary, eminently serviceable in that it
offered his contemporaries an image which they themselves found
supportive – and which provides today's readers with a timely reminder
that Non-standard Englishes are markers of infinite variety and value, in
English culture past and present.

To begin with, the poetry (the work in Dorset dialect and also that in
Standard English) is not trivially sentimental: Barnes' depth of feeling
for people and places and his distress at their passing is profound. 'The
wife a-lost' (333), for example, is a simple, moving tribute – 'Since I
noo mwore do zee your feäce' – to his own wife Julia, who died after
twenty-five years of marriage. And 'Dawn' is an intensely sad elegy for
lost friends and lost visions: the sun may rise day after day, but it
'comes not to shine / On any early friends of mine' (933). Nor was
Barnes so concerned with his declared aim to 'light up [the country-
side's] more lovely features' (1841: 510–11) that his poetry totally
ignores the shadows of poverty and of destructive nineteenth-century
change.

Instead it confronts, particularly in its eclogues, the impoverish-
ment of the labourer as he loses his livelihood through enclosure,
engrossing and increased mechanization. And it regrets the indignities
consequently suffered through the Poor Law Amendment Act, and
the severing of family ties as younger members emigrate to find
work.[1]

> 'Tis hard a man can't eärn a lwoaf to veed 'en
> Upon the pleäce wher life wer vust a-gi'ed en;
> An' hard that when he'd work there's noo work vor'n,
> ('Over sea to settle', 485)

Furthermore, although as a professional and travelled man Barnes'
own horizons broadened well beyond Dorset, he mistrusted encroaching
city life. He did not like its 'pent aïr' ('Sound o' water', 311), or its
'peevish meäster' ('My orcha'd in Linden Lea', 233). And he did not
like its economy, buying up farm land, new landlords destroying the old
ways of rural life.

Vor to catch at land, Thomas, an' snatch at land,
   Now is the plan;
Meäke money wherever you can.

('The leäne', 306)

Traditions were being destroyed, and these included the local language. Thomas Hardy (who had first met Barnes when apprenticed to
his Dorchester neighbour as an architect) confirmed, in his introduction
to a selection of the poems, that the dialect was 'fast-perishing' even as
Barnes chose it for his poems (1908: viii). Of course, all languages alter
gradually and inevitably as society alters. English has Germanic
origins, but over the centuries has picked up traces of Latin and French.
Along the way it has altered its sound. Between the time of Chaucer and
Shakespeare there was a 'Great Vowel Shift' and even Shakespeare –
pronouncing *weak* and *week* differently, and making *oc-ce-an* trisyllabic
– would have seemed odd to our ears. But in Barnes' lifetime spreading
education and industrial changes were accelerating the process of
change. W.A. Wright called for the foundation of a society to preserve
Non-standard dialects, arguing that 'In a few years it will be too late.
Railroads and certificated teachers are doing their work' (1870: 271).
Hardy reflected the fact in his fictional Tess Durbeyfield. Tess attended
a National School in her village (one of those set up in early Victorian
Britain by the National Society for Promoting the Education of the Poor
in the Principles of the Established Church) and having 'passed the
Sixth Standard ... under a London-trained mistress, spoke two lan-
guages; the dialect at home, more or less; ordinary English abroad and
to persons of quality' (Hardy 1974 edition: 48). However, even
speaking the dialect only 'more or less' was anathema to those
Victorians who considered themselves 'truly genteel': in Hardy's *The
Mayor of Casterbridge* they labelled dialect words 'those terrible marks
of the beast' (Hardy 1978 edition: 200).

So, when Barnes regrets the passing of beloved voices in 'The vaïces
that be gone', he is overtly regretting the loss of friends and family,
through change and through death. But the poem is also emblematic of
this other kind of loss: the passing of the sounds and sentiments of the
Vale of Blackmore's distinctive voice, a variety of English which
Barnes sought to commemorate, not only through his 'rural English'
poems but also through academic discussion in a number of publications (including a 'Dissertation' to be found in the 1844 and 1847
editions of his *Poems of Rural Life*).[2] His desire to preserve the dialect's
'old song' seems encapsulated in another of his poems – this time,
ironically, a Standard English poem – 'Sing again together'.

Sing again together

Since now, once more beside this mound,
We friends are here below the limes,
Come, let us try if we can sound
A song we sang in early times.

When out among the hay in mead
Or o'er the fields, or down the lane,
Our Jenny's voice would gaily lead
The others, chiming strain by strain.

When roses' buds are all outblown,
The lilies' cups will open white;
When lilies' cups at last are flown,
The later pinks unfold to sight.

We learnt good songs that came out new
But now are old among the young,
And after we are gone, but few
Will know the songs that we have sung.

So let us sing another rhyme
On this old mound in summer time.

(751)

Barnes' choice of the Standard dialect for this and other poems demonstrates not only his desire that future Standard-speaking generations should be acquainted with the language and themes of old songs that once were sung, but also his ambivalence towards the new songs. He seems to accept that new language, sometimes Standard language, inevitably supersedes the old: all language changes over time just as the 'later pinks' naturally replace the roses and the lilies' cups. Moreover, the later pinks may be just as lovely as the roses' buds, and songs that come out new are always good in the estimation of their own generation.

Barnes' complex attitude to changing language will be returned to in due course. But, for the moment, suffice it to say that he appeared to see in his dialect poetry, with its thematic and linguistic preservation of the past, a necessary thread of stabilizing continuity for future generations. In this way, his poems fulfil a similar function to the paths, mills, towers, bridges and houses which Barnes prized because, built and left behind by earlier generations – 'our fathers' works' – they continued to mark the landscape and to be of use to new generations. He urged

Zoo now mid nwone ov us vorget
The pattern our vorefathers zet;
But each be faïn to underteäke
Zome work to meäke vor others' gaïn,
That we mid leäve mwore good to sheäre
Less ills to beäre, less souls to grieve

(270)

But why exactly, in the face of opposition to its 'marks of the beast' (so-called in Hardy's fiction and implied by many in reality), did Barnes believe so firmly that the dialect was a vital and worthwhile part of the traditional pattern?

THE 'MAGIC CIRCLES' OF DIALECTS

Pressure to refine and standardize English was not new in the nineteenth century. Four hundred years previously William of Malmesbury, according to Caxton's *The Description of Britain* (1480), despaired of northerners' English. He thought it would have been much improved if only royalty had left London more often, giving subjects in far-flung regions the benefit of their king's English. Then, in 1712, Jonathan Swift published *A Proposal for Correcting, Improving and Ascertaining the English Tongue*, bringing to a head long-considered proposals for the establishment of an academy to control and fix the language.

In fact, up to a point, Barnes might have supported Swift's un-realized aims. For Swift was partly motivated by a desire to secure wide communication and the permanency of written records and Barnes, as a teacher, prized lucid and widely accessible language. In fact, despite his love for the local dialect, he spoke and taught his own pupils in a form of Standard English. Still, he would have resisted the establishment of a single standard, set for the many by the influential few, those whose writings, if Swift had had his way, 'might probably be preserved with Care, and grow into Esteem, and the Authors have a chance for Immortality' (quoted in Crowley 1991: 33). For Barnes was not convinced that Standard English was unquestionably the best English.

After all, it does not even have the merit of archetypal purity. It too is a dialect. It began as one of a number of English varieties, the East Midlands dialect, spoken in and around London at the end of the medieval period. But, started in this powerhouse and spread in gradually altering form by revered nobility and wealthy merchants, the Standard's influence has been maintained by the powerful and the prestigious. Yet, in Barnes' opinion it had become by the nineteenth century a language 'fit only for learned people to converse with each other in', clogged with obscure vocabulary which he tried to purge from the Standard variety he used in his own classroom (1830: 501–3).[3]

Besides, in his view, the Standard's upper-class and learned speakers had their limitations. For example, Barnes despaired that those who had 'had their lots cast in town-occupations of a highly civilized community' could not appreciate the 'rustic mind' believing that 'every change from the plough towards the desk and from the desk towards the couch of empty handed idleness is an onward step towards happiness and intellectual and moral excellence' (1847: 49). So he always feared that the poems he wrote about Dorset life in Standard English would, though more widely accessible than his dialect work, be misunderstood by these town-bred readers.

In order to prevent the ignorance of standardization and to fully appreciate other minds including the rural – which, in Barnes' view, was at least as 'full of wisdom and goodness' (1844: Preface) as the mentality of the city – outsiders would need to come to terms with varieties of English apart from their own. Barnes would have been familiar with the work of the German linguist, Wilhelm von Humboldt, who had suggested (anticipating the Whorfian hypothesis discussed in chapters 1 and 4) that each different language draws a 'magic circle' round the people who speak it. There is no 'escape' from our own inherited circle, wrote Humboldt, except 'by stepping out of it into another' (in Cassirer 1946: 9). Now, a dialect can, in its strangeness, seem like a wholly foreign language but, if its circle is willingly entered, infinite riches may be discovered in its unusual sounds and rhythms, words and syntax.

These are the riches of local identity and special, local understanding. For each dialect has, in its idiosyncrasies, the quality that Gerard Manley Hopkins, Barnes' contemporary, would have termed *inscape*, a distinctiveness which, in its turn, can express the special, distinct inscape of the people and places to which it belongs, revealing what Hopkins called their *instress*, an underlying force which shapes and maintains their individuality. It would seem that Barnes held a similar view and mourned the passing of the local voice, believing it to be an expression of localness. He wished, he said, to give Blackmore people 'a poetry of their own' (1841: 510–11) and would have been delighted to know that Hopkins believed his use of Dorset English 'heightens [the poems'] effect': 'it is as if', wrote Hopkins, 'Dorset life and Dorset landscape had taken flesh and tongue in the man' (in Abbott 1955: 85–9, 220–2).

Local audiences evidently agreed. Barnes' daughter, Lucy Baxter (writing as Leader Scott), noted that when Barnes read his work aloud it seemed

> that the crowd of human beings was a magic harp on which [he] played, bringing forth at his will the emotions he chose. If this seems exaggerated, let it be remembered that it was the first time a Dorset audience had heard its feelings, language, and daily life portrayed in its own common speech.

> (Scott 1887: 167)

Nevertheless, although today, in his birthplace, Barnes' poetry is still much loved and 'sung again', relatively few outside the Vale of Blackmore have been drawn into the circle of his poems and have appreciated the inscape of their unusual language. However, recent educational developments might have encouraged others to recognize the special value of the poetry's particular phonology, lexicon and syntax. For though – like Barnes himself in his own school – government directives in the late 1980s advocated the teaching of Standard English first and foremost, they did not decry all other varieties of the language. Indeed, they advocated an 'explicit' understanding of language which, if achieved, could facilitate appreciation of English in all its rich variation.

AN 'EXPLICIT' UNDERSTANDING

Sir John Kingman's *Report of the Committee of Inquiry into the Teaching of English* (1988: 14) and subsequent government directives argued that every child, whatever the variety of English spoken at home, has a *right* to acquire Standard English syntax and lexicon. However, the rationale was one of pragmatism, not of superiority. For a child can hardly be denied proficiency in a variety which has become a prescribed norm, essential for interaction and acceptance beyond the immediate family and community.

In fact, a majority of us have always been taught to write Standard English and if it is not our family's variety we may, like Hardy's Tess, speak its words and syntax in addition to a local variety. Even so, we may not choose the so-called RP (Received Pronunciation) accent, the accent which is not related to any particular region of England but which tends to be associated with an upper class. Instead, most of us team our Standard syntax and lexicon with a local pronunciation. But we may do so with misgivings, for research has shown people critical not only of others' ways of speaking but also of their own Non-standard sounds (Honey 1989: 60).

This is hardly surprising. For the powerful and prestigious have not simply assumed that Standard lexicon, syntax and RP accent comprise the only correct and properly expressive form of English for themselves, they have also prescribed it for everyone else. Anthony Lejeune (*Daily Telegraph*, 1 January 1985) argued that the words and grammar of Standard English are 'the mortar which hold our thoughts together', insisting that when 'they crumble, so does our capacity for thought', and Norman Tebbitt appeared to imply that a failure to teach children Standard syntax above all other grammars would set them on the road to crime (Radio Four, November 1985; see Bain 1991)!

Similar notions of 'Standard' excellence evidently extend beyond the English border, for the poet Tom Leonard's Non-standard Scottish-English speaker is almost persuaded of his own linguistic short-comings.

> right inuff
> ma language is disgraceful
>
> ma maw tellt mi
> ma teacher tellt mi
> thi doactir tellt mi
> thi priest tellt mi
>
> ma boss tellt me

And, even,

> sum wee smout thit thoat ah hudny read chomsky tellt mi

But then – because he *has* read Chomsky – he decides on reflection that

> all livin language is sacred
> fuck thi lohta thim
>   (Leonard 1984: 120)

And the American linguist, Noam Chomsky himself, might not disagree. For he has long emphasized the structured, 'rule-based' nature of language – *all* languages and all varieties of language – explaining that each human being is born, regardless of gender, race or class, to the same capacity for infinite language creativity through systems of rules.

True, the language performance of an individual varies according to the kind of language inherited by his or her social and familial group, and according to each context of use and to personal preference. But variations towards the Standard cannot be automatically equated with effective communication. Standard English can, elegantly or inelegantly, express logic or illogic, wisdom or stupidity. One well-known experiment, described by the American sociolinguist, William Labov (1969), contrasts the ineffective, illogical, verbose and banal use of Standard American English by a college-educated Black American with the Non-standard, yet infinitely more expressive, imaginative and logical language of a Harlem street-gang teenager.

Barnes would not have been surprised and he would have been relieved to know that, despite Kingman's insistence on a child's right to the Standard, the Report, recognizing the perspectives of linguists like Chomsky and Labov, acknowledged the considerable value and importance of all varieties of language. Barnes would have welcomed its insistence that each and every variety 'has its own authenticity' (1988: 7) of which users may be 'rightly proud' (1988: 14), and its acknowledgement that all varieties have 'richness' and a psychological importance as expressions of personal identity and of ties within family and peer groups (1988: 14).

For Kingman, then, Standard words and syntax should be *added* to the repertoires of those who arrive at school using a different variety, rather than forced as a replacement. As for Non-standard accents, these should, in Kingman's view, be left unchallenged.

Furthermore, the Kingman Report stressed that children should know *why* alternatives to the Standard are to be respected. They should have an informed response to those who thoughtlessly reject them, and have their own considered answers to questions like the one raised in John Honey's book title: *Does Accent Matter*? For, whilst the generalized language awareness encouraged in the classrooms of the 1960s to the 1980s was valuable in its encouragement of creative speech and writing, Kingman suggests it is incomplete without an *explicit* (1988: 12) understanding of the systems and social uses of language. Five and six year olds are hardly likely to read the work of seminal grammarians or sociolinguists, like Chomsky or Labov, but the National Curriculum has required the provision of such linguistic knowledge in appropriate forms as soon as possible.

If this knowledge is acquired, English speakers who have both Standard and Non-standard English in their repertoire could, in theory, range between their alternatives, deliberately choosing for themselves the variety of English they find most communicative in a particular context. At the very least they might not reject the unusualness of another speaker's choice but appreciate its specialness of form and expression. They might, in the process, confirm the Arabic proverb of which Barnes approved: 'A man by learning a second language becomes two.'

Unfortunately, however, this broadening of linguistic understanding and appreciation may not now take place. For at the time of writing, National Curriculum requirements are to alter once more. A much narrower approach to the teaching of English, requiring the Standard variety to be used in the classroom, and moreover in the playground, is being demanded. Students may not, then, have the opportunity to give due consideration to alternative varieties – in effect, to 'second languages'.

A MAN BY LEARNING A SECOND LANGUAGE BECOMES TWO

The lexicon, grammar and phonology of the nineteenth-century Vale of Blackmoor dialect are all distinctive – in a sense a second language to the Standard English speaker. But readers entering its circle may appreciate Barnes' poems as if they were themselves members of the Blackmore community. Take, to begin with, the lexicon.

Lexicon

The vocabulary of the dialect poems is certainly unusual and its strangeness naturally gives to them an immediate local flavour – what Hopkins would have called inscape. There is *bibber* for 'shiver', *caddle* for 'mix up', *veag* for a 'fit of anger'. But some words are not so easily and directly translated. When apples *happer* in Barnes' poetry it is not sufficient to guess from surrounding language that they simply fall: the word means, according to Barnes' own Glossary (1847), 'to fall so hard as to hop up . . . as hailstones or rain-drops from ground or pavement in a hard storm'.

Perhaps little of significance is lost if this is not realized, but other misunderstandings could be much more significant. Barnes begins 'Sound o' water' (311) with the lines

I born in town! oh no my dawn
O' life broke here bezide theäse lawn;
Not where pent aïr do roll along,
In darkness drough the wall-bound drong,

These lines will be completely misunderstood and trivialized if it is automatically assumed – as it might well be by the Standard English reader – that *lawn* means a smooth, well kept sweep of garden. In fact, for Barnes' community it meant unploughed land in a field – no hint of comfortable suburbia here. Moreover, if we do not know that *drong* could mean both a narrow way and a throng of people we cannot fully sense the close, crowded city lanes, their claustrophobia disliked and even feared by those accustomed to open-air field work.

Still, Non-standard lexicons may be accepted by Standard speakers as 'quaint'. Resistance to Non-standard grammar is usually stronger. Indeed, there is an assumption that Non-standard Englishes do not even have grammar, and instead utter sloppy, irregular and therefore inexpressive versions of 'proper' English syntax. Barnes' poetry demonstrates, however, that a variety is, by definition, consistent in its particular syntactic patterns, as well as in its lexicon and its phonology: it is, in Chomskyan terms, as grammatically rule-governed as the Standard – but the rules, of course, are different.

Structure and meaning

Take, for example, the first unusual-sounding word in 'The vaïces that be gone': *plaÿsome*. Dorset had the morphological rule, noun + *some* = adjective. But Barnes explains in his Dissertation (1844) that words formed with the suffix *some* do not imply the same meaning as words formed by the Standard derivational rule, noun + *ful* = adjective. He argued that whilst *ful* means 'having much of a thing', *some* implies *apt to do*. *Plaÿsome* is therefore more logical than *playful*, for in Barnes' view a flight, being an action, cannot *possess* play – but it may be apt to play. It is a fine distinction, but no less valid than Lejeune's objection (*Daily Telegraph*, 1 January 1985) that *regretfully* does not mean the same as *regrettably*, and it is a small proof of the complexity and subtlety that the hostile do not recognize in Non-standard language. True, it is a different 'mortar' from Lejeune's (referred to earlier in this chapter) but it is evidently just as effective as the Standard in holding thoughts.

A more important semantic distinction, however, lies in the Dorset use of the auxiliary verb *do/did*. It implies continuity, a continuing state of affairs which, in Standard English, would have to be expressed by the addition of an adverb or the phrase *used to*. 'Where the birds did zing' thus implies they *used to* do so *regularly*. It is important to recognize this small distinction in order to appreciate the precise inscape of Barnes' work, for the auxiliary's constant use, over and over in his poetry, contributes – if acknowledged – to the sense of consistent security with which he invests his image of time past: the sun always shone, friends always met, flowers always bloomed.

But the Dorset use of this auxiliary has, in Barnes' poems, a further significance connected with the sounds he chose to emphasize.

Sound and meaning

The regular use of unstressed *did* and *do* produces longer phrases than Standard syntax, and slows and steadies rhythm. It therefore contributes to the tranquility and (Barnes' word) 'mellowness' which pervades the poems. But the auxiliary's role in producing what Hertz calls 'a masterpiece of orchestration . . . [an] all-encompassing euphony' (1985: 113) is played in combination with other regular features including the prefix *a*. Words like *a-laugh'd* and *a-gone* are not products of a lazy tongue, as detractors might believe, but begin with an affix which, according to Barnes' explanation in his Dissertation (1844), is a descendant of the Anglo-Saxon *ge-*. It too lengthens, slows and smooths.

The Dorset suffix *-en*, (*a-playen*), can also smooth and ease because its closing consonant /n/ may, more readily than the /ŋ/ of Standard *-ing*, lend itself to elision with a following consonant.

Vowels too are important in achieving what Hertz called a 'honeyed slowness' (1985: 113). Dorset frequently pronounces one between two consonants that, in Standard English, are not divided: so *elem* tree is lengthened and seems to roll more smoothly off the tongue. There are, besides, a considerable number of diaereses, both of two adjacent vowels being individually sounded (as in 'aïr'), drawing out the pronunciation of a word.

Barnes believed the 'mellowness' he signified in these ways was 'sometimes wanting in the national language' and, also, a particularly 'good vehicle' for the local personality's 'softer feelings' (1844: Dissertation). But every personality in Dorchester could hardly have been mellow and gentle! Yet it was the aspect of identity Barnes wished to emphasize in order to produce a poetry that he believed was 'sound, and high toned' (1841: 510–11). In fact, he altered lines between their first and last publications during his lifetime in ways which increase their softness and musicality.

A line from 'The spring' (71) began in 1844 as 'An' we can hear birds zing, and zee', but in 1847 became 'When birds da zing, an' we can zee', a version which sounds more softly undulating, probably because the two occurrences of stressed /z/ are separated by a further stress, one which, moreover, adds a second gentle glide, /w/. Finally, in 1879, 'da' is replaced with the rather longer-sounding vowel of 'do'.

Yet a mellow tone is not the impression given by every dialect poem Barnes wrote. Take, for example, the eclogue 'Rusticus emigrans' (482). The consonants of the following extract (/t/, /d/, /n/, /m/, /k/, /g/ and so on) produce a comparatively disjointed and harsh-sounding utterance – as well they might, considering the import of the exchange.

ROBERT Well Richat, zoo 'tis true what I do hear
That you be guoin to Dieman's Land to-year.

RICHARD Ees, I shall never eat another pound
O' zalt in England here, where I wer barn;
Nor dig another spit o'English ground;
Nor cut a bit muore English grass or carn.

Yet even this poem eventually takes on the familiar luxuriant richness of sound and rhythm. For later Richard lists – with vowels that are stressed, longish and so (as in 'here', 'trees', 'buones', for instance) contribute to the rhythm of an incantation – all that has been precious in his environment.

Here be the trees that I did use to clim in,
Here is the brook that I did use to zwim in,
Here be the ground where I've a worked and played;
Here is the hut that I wer barn and bred in;
Here is the little church where we've a prayed,
And churchyard that my kinsvolk's buones be laid in.

All in all, then, Barnes' dialect poetry is an answer to those who despair that the Non-standard is, by comparison with the Standard, an ungrammatical, inexpressive, unartistic sham, to those who perhaps equate the Non-standard with 'street speech', defined as 'unformed, ignorant, punctuated by the pulsing minimalist obscenities of people with starveling vocabularies whose speech curses their condition' (*Guardian*, 31 October 1990: 21).

Of course, this attack could as easily be aimed at Standard English: Standard speakers are not automatically exempt from ignorance or without obscenity. And it is not clear whether the comment means street speech swears *at* its users' condition, or the speech itself makes their condition damnable. Still, Non-standard English which does curse its speakers' condition can certainly be found – and in poetry. Indeed, in confronting human frailties and hardship Tennyson's Lincolnshire monologues may have a special appeal for those who believe Barnes did his particular audiences a dishonest disservice in avoiding the harsh side of the labouring life. But, yet again, the use of the Non-standard, in art of this kind, confirms that it is not automatically synonymous with 'unformed' and 'ignorant' street speech.

For C.H. Sisson is, I think, mistaken when he argues (1965: 44) that the Lincolnshire language is not so well rendered as the sounds and syntax of Tennyson's more usual poetry. True, the familiar mellifluous Tennyson is not here. And the Standard language of Victorian gentility is ignored. But instead there is the sound, word and grammar of a tough honesty that is perfectly managed within the traditional – 'standard' – forms of poetry. Tennyson's skilful and creative use of language is merely adapted from its usual to an unusual variety of English.

Each of his seven monologues, published between 1861 and 1892 (Ricks 1969), expresses the unvarnished feelings of a local personality in unvarnished local language. Indeed, the poems generally grew out of remarks that Tennyson had heard, first or second hand, around Spilsby, where he was brought up. 'The village wife', for example, grew out of a sentence attributed to the Tennysons' own cook and apparently referring to the Tennysons themselves: 'If you raäked out hell wi' a small-tooth coämb you wouldn't find their likes' (Campion 1969: v).

The lines of the monologues are mostly rhyming couplets, end-stopped. They are long, jagged with chunky, pithy phrases and a dogged beat. Their rhymes are generally short, sharp and heavily stressed. So the poetry 'behaves' like its personae – rough, forthright, vigorous and much more contrary than Barnes' people but, like Barnes' Dorset families, not without intelligence, clarity or self-awareness.

Hear, for instance, a cantankerous spinster spit out, with the utmost precision, her distaste for children.

> But I niver not wished for childer, I hevn't na likin fur brats;
> Pretty anew when ya dresses 'em oop, an' they goas fur a walk,
> Or sits wi' their 'ands afoor 'em, an' doesn't not 'inder the talk!
> But their bottles o' pap, an' their mucky bibs, an' the clats an' the clouts,
> An' their mashin their toys to pieaces an' maakin ma deaf wi' their shouts,
>
> (Ricks 1969: 1327, 84–8)

This diatribe's plosives and harsh consonant combinations force upon the reader's eyes and ears the dirt and disruption of real life. There is no room here for the sentimental – and clean – images of Victoriana before the spinster eventually breaks off to attend to her cats, those 'sweet-arts' whom she appreciates so much more than husbands or children.

Both Tennyson and Barnes have, therefore, in their very different ways, preserved and dignified Non-standard varieties of English. Their dialect poems might profitably be taught in English classrooms not only for their intrinsic value as art but also as an antidote to prejudice, a reinforcement and exemplification of some of the 'explicit' and sensitive linguistic awareness urged by Kingman and an extension of the repertoires of those who do not speak these varieties of English.

Nevertheless, Barnes did not write exclusively in Blackmore dialect.

And it is something of a puzzle that, given his firm belief in the match between local language and local people, Barnes demonstrated the ambivalence referred to earlier in this chapter and ended his life writing about Dorset life mostly in Standard English. Perhaps he felt that his particular dialect's use, as a symbol of localness and local value, was becoming too obviously anachronistic as populations moved, and as tones and syntax altered and became more standardized. Perhaps he felt that the images of 'wisdom and goodness', which he continued to write, would reach more people in the Standard form – though, as already noted, he was not certain that their sentiments would be readily appreciated by Standard speakers. Perhaps he needed it to express his own personality, for he himself used the Standard in many areas of his life and the later poems do seem to have more in them of Barnes himself and rather less of the labouring family's day-to-day existence.

Whatever the precise reason, from time to time in his life Barnes actually translated some of his dialect work into what he called 'common' English. 'Sing again together' (751), quoted above, was made (together with 'Season tokens' (752), given in suggestions for further work at the end of this chapter) from an earlier dialect poem 'Zing together oonce mwore' (555). The existence of both the Blackmore version and those in Standard, 'common' English provide an opportunity to assess their comparative effectiveness.

However, this chapter ends with the original version – with its 'inscape' of fellowship and sunshine preserving the height of summer, the prime of life and the local voice even as the light changed and shadows fell – that Barnes must have hoped, despite the increasing power of the Standard, 'we midden quite vorget'.

Zing together oonce mwore

Since here, bezide the hangen's brow,
We friends be all ageän a-met,
We'll zee if we've a-left us now
A zong we midden quite vorget;
A ditty we, in down an' meäd,
Or out in vield, or up the drong,
Did zing, as oone did gaïly leäd,
An' others all come in so strong;
A ditty we, in all our prime
O' life, did zing in zummer time,
While sheädes may show the time ov day,
The flow'rs how zummer wanes away.
Where thyme on tufty banks did grow,

Or mallows on the leänezide ledge,
About the blue-barr'd geäte, did show
Their grey-blue heads bezide the hedge;
Or where the poppy's scarlet crown
Did nod by clover, dusky red;
Or where the leäze wer ruddy-brown,
By brooks wi' shallow-water'd bed,
We there, all merry, zide by zide,
Did zing along in zummer tide;
An' where the light o' dyen day
So softly on the walls did sheen,
Below the slopen thatch, brown-grey,
By slopen ground o' peälish green,
Or where, in grass all zummer dried,
Did show the thistle's purple studs,
An' beds o' dandelions plied
Their stems wi' yollow fringed buds,
As we in tuen, rhyme by rhyme,
Did zing our zongs in zummer time.
When rwoses' buds have all a-blown,
The lily cups do open white;
When lily cups be all a-vlown,
The leäter pinks do come to zight.
The ditties we did leaärn so new
Be over-wold among the young;
When we be all a-gone, but vew
Will know the zongs that we've a-zung.
Zoo let us zing another rhyme
Or two here now in zummer time.

(555)

SUGGESTIONS FOR FURTHER WORK

1 Compare 'Zing together oonce mwore' (555), quoted above, with the two poems 'translated' from it, 'Sing again together' (751), also quoted above, and 'Season tokens' (752), given below.

Season tokens

The shades may show the time of day,
And flowers how summer wanes away.

Where thyme on turfy banks may grow,

Or mallows by the laneside ledge,
About the blue-barr'd gate, may show
Their grey-blue heads beside the hedge,
Or where the poppy's scarlet crown
May nod by clover, dusky red,
Or where the field is ruddy brown,
By brooks with shallow-water'd bed,

The shades may show the time of day,
And flowers how summer wanes away.

Or, where the light of dying day
May softly shine against the wall,
Below the sloping thatch, brown-grey,
Or over pale-green grass, may fall,
Or where, in fields that heat burns dry,
May show the thistle's purple studs,
Or beds of dandelions ply
Their stems with yellow fringed buds,

There shades may show the time of day,
And flowers how summer wanes away.

First, identify and describe as carefully as possible the differences you find in the versions' sounds, words and syntax. Then, bearing in mind these differences, consider the following questions.

Do the Dorset dialect versions seem to you as expressive as the Standard poems? Do they seem any more effective as 'poetry of their own' (i.e. poetry of the Blackmore people) than the Standard versions? Do the Standard ones seem more the voice of the vicar, schoolmaster and grammarian that Barnes had become?

2 Consider Hardy's ironic view of attitudes to Standard and Non-standard English as markers of class in his poem 'The ruined maid' (Gibson 1976: 158).

7 The language of women and men

'Nervous prostration', by Anna Wickham with particular reference to Jonathan Swift's 'The furniture of a woman's mind'

This chapter discusses possible differences between female and male uses of language and a variety of attitudes to these differences. Some of the issues discussed here, together with other perspectives on gender and language, are the subject of papers in The Feminist Critique of Language *(Cameron 1990).*

CHATTER, NATTER, PRATTLE, BITCH, WHINE . . .

The Furniture of a Woman's Mind

Written in the Year 1727

A Set of Phrases learn't by Rote;
·A Passion for a Scarlet-Coat;
When at a Play to laugh, or cry,
Yet cannot tell the Reason why:
Never to hold her Tongue a Minute;
While all she prates has nothing in it.
Whole Hours can with a Coxcomb sit,
And take his Nonsense all for Wit:
Her Learning mounts to read a Song,
But, half the Words pronouncing wrong;
Has ev'ry Repartee in Store,
She spoke ten Thousand Times before.
Can ready Compliments supply
On all Occasions, cut and dry.
Such Hatred to a Parson's Gown,
The Sight will put her in a Swown.
For Conversation well endu'd;
She calls it witty to be rude;

And, placing Raillery in Railing,
Will tell aloud your greatest Failing;
Nor makes a Scruple to expose
Your bandy Leg, or crooked Nose.
Can, at her Morning Tea, run o'er
The Scandal of the Day before.
Improving hourly in her Skill,
To cheat and wrangle at Quadrille.

In chusing Lace a Critick nice,
Knows to a Groat the lowest Price;
Can in her Female Clubs dispute
What Lining best the Silk wil suit;
What Colours each Complexion match
And where with Art to place a Patch.

If chance a Mouse creeps in her Sight,
Can finely counterfeit a Fright;
So, sweetly screams if it comes near her,
She ravishes all Hearts to hear her.
Can dext'rously her Husband teize,
By taking Fits whene'er she please:
By frequent Practice learns the Trick
At proper Seasons to be sick;
Thinks nothing gives one Airs so pretty;
At once creating Love and Pity.
If *Molly* happens to be careless,
And but neglects to warm her Hair-Lace,
She gets a Cold as sure as Death;
And vows she scarce can fetch her Breath.
Admires how modest Women can
Be so *robustious* like a man.

In Party, furious to her Power;
A bitter Whig, or Tory sow'r;
Her Arguments directly tend
Against the Side she would defend:
Will prove herself a Tory plain,
From Principles the Whigs maintain;
And, to defend the Whiggish Cause,
Her Topicks from the Tories draws.

Oh yes! If any Man can find
More virtues in a Woman's Mind,

Let them be sent to Mrs *Harding*;
She'll pay the Charges to a Farthing:
Take Notice, she has my Commission
To add them in the next Edition;
They may out-sell a better Thing;
So, Holla Boys; God save the King.
                    (Williams 1958: 415–18)

Western society believes, suggests Cora Kaplan (1986, reprinted in
Cameron 1990: 57–69, 63), that women, like children, should be seen
but not heard. Jacques Lacan, the late French psychoanalyst, offered an
interpretation of Freudian theory that might explain this sorry state of
affairs.[1] Children are acquiring language around the Oedipal stage and,
in his view, whilst boys assume maleness and at the same time mastery
of the language, girls recognize their difference and eventually become
women of restricted speech in the shadow of the linguistic order's
patriarchal preference. Whether or not this unequal development is
essential and immutable is debatable, but it is arguably an historical
symptom. For women have not always been encouraged to talk, at least
not to do so with any authority. As Donovan points out (in Cameron
1990: 42), girls were denied access to the Latinate education that, until
the seventeenth century and beyond, prepared men for a public, formal
platform. True, women gained a voice in literature with their contribution to the eighteenth-century rise of the novel – a new form that did not
depend on the old Latinate rhetoric. But, as Spencer points out (1986:
xi), 'women's writing is not the same as women's rights' and 'the
feminisation of literature defined literature as a special category
supposedly outside the political arena, with an influence on the world as
indirect as women's was supposed to be'. Women remained as children,
pretty to look at, engaging and charming, but their intellectual views
would be of little consequence to adult – male – society. If their voices
were heard they might be effectively silenced through ridicule, after the
eighteenth-century fashion of Jonathan Swift. His poem, 'The furniture
of a woman's mind', sniggered that a woman prated politics with
arguments that 'directly tend / Against the side she would defend'.

But it has not been woman's public voice alone that has been
trivialized. 'The furniture of a woman's mind' sneers at female
discourse in general – just as, Coates argues in *Women, Men and
Language* (1986: 16–34), men have done for centuries.

In the opinion of such men, she explains, women have always used
the wrong words, poor grammar and generally talked too much.
Moreover, men were grumbling two hundred years before Swift's poem

that nannies taught noblemen's children a 'corrupte and foul' pronunciation (Elyot 1531) and 'The furniture of a woman's mind' is no more complimentary: though it concedes that women were able to read, it complains they did so whilst 'half the words pronouncing wrong'.

As for conversation, to Swift's ear women merely regurgitated a 'set of phrases learnt by rote', full of 'ready compliments . . . cut and dry', their repartee repeated 'ten thousand times before'. In 1711 he had written elsewhere, in *Thoughts on Various Subjects* (Hayward 1949), that such automatic fluency was not to be admired. He seemed to find speech hesitancy a generally male characteristic and no disgrace but, rather, proof of a rich multiplicity of ideas waiting for selection: 'common speakers' on the other hand 'have only one set of ideas, and one set of words to clothe them in; and these are always ready at the mouth' (Hayward 1949: 21). True, he admitted that men might be amongst these 'common' speakers, but he seemed to think the culprits were more likely to be female for he noted that a 'very little Wit is valued in a Woman; as we are pleased with a few Words spoken plain by a Parrot' (Hayward 1949: 24).

So, empty-headed woman was, regrettably in Swift's opinion, 'Never to hold her tongue a minute' and always prattled about fabrics, complexions and patches – evidently light-weight trivia in comparison with the eighteenth-century equivalent of men's present-day debates on sport, cars and page 3. No wonder silence has always been thought golden – by men, for women and children. Still, given the poem's own smug ridicule, is it not hypocritical for it to complain if woman 'calls it witty to be rude' and 'Will tell aloud your greatest failing'? Perhaps, after all, Swift should not be taken at face value. Maybe his poem is another spoof of his 'Modest proposal' proportions, the essay written in 1729 (Hayward 1949: 427–35) in which his imaginary 'projector' advises 'persons of quality and fortune' to buy and to eat impoverished Irish children in order to prevent them 'from Being a Burden to Their Parents or Country' and to make them 'Beneficial to the Public'. If so, perhaps Swift intended the poem's coxcomb, whose 'nonsense' women were inclined to 'take all for wit', to be an (unconscious) self-portrait of its persona. In which case, all *I* myself prate here 'has nothing in it'.

But then, whilst no reader in their right mind is likely to harbour a penchant for cannibalism, and the intended irony of 'Modest proposal' is therefore indisputable, can male readers of the poem be counted on to spot an outrageous sexist joke and leap to their women's defence? It seems unlikely, given their traditional ridicule of women's talk and the widespread present-day use of verbs like *chatter, natter, prattle, whine* to indicate 'girl' talk. Besides, the crispness of the poem's couplets' neat and perfect rhymes, and the jaunty regularity of their rhythm, trumpet the confident sexism which is a forerunner of Music Hall wit and a (milder?) version of today's Club comedy. Their cruel word cartoons build, image after image, a picture that may, like mother-in-law jokes, be just too simplistically funny for an audience to question. Without reflection, assessment or sensible qualification, damning statements pile inexorably one upon the other. They are apparently the premises that entail the poem's vacuous conclusion in a reaffirmation of male solidarity and power – 'So, holla boys; God Save the King'.

If this is a model – even a parody – of genuine male logic, past and present, it is not surprising to hear Luce Irigaray, the French psychoanalyst, insist that 'within an Aristotelian type of logic ... which dominates our most everyday statements' women's essential natures cannot articulate themselves unless as an 'undertone' (Cameron 1990: 82).

Anna Wickham, in her poem 'Nervous prostration', appears to share a great deal of twentieth-century thinking on these lines, contrasting an emotional, female, life and language with repressed and repressive male behaviour.

LANGUAGE USE AND ABUSE

Nervous prostration

I married a man of the Croydon class
When I was twenty-two.
And I vex him, and he bores me
Till we don't know what to do!
It isn't good form in the Croydon class
To say you love your wife,
So I spend my days with the tradesmen's books
And pray for the end of life.

In green fields are blossoming trees
And a golden wealth of gorse,
And young birds sing for joy of worms:
It's perfectly clear, of course,
That it wouldn't be taste in the Croydon class
To sing over dinner or tea:
But I sometimes wish the gentleman
Would turn and talk to me!

But every man of the Croydon class
Lives in terror of joy and speech.
'Words are betrayers', 'Joys are brief' –
The maxims their wise ones teach –
And for all my labour of love and life
I shall be clothed and fed,
And they'll give me an orderly funeral
When I'm still enough to be dead.

I married a man of the Croydon class
When I was twenty-two
And I vex him, and he bores me
Till we don't know what to do!
And as I sit in his ordered house,
I feel I must sob or shriek,
To force a man of the Croydon class
To live, or to love, or to speak!
(Smith 1984: 210, first published in *The Man with a Hammer*, 1916)

Joy, love and life itself are, for the poem's speaker, linked intimately
with the use of language. It seems to her the most natural thing that
living should be both deeply felt *and* expressed. After all, in stanza 2,
birds, fields, plants and trees communicate themselves and their
essential natures in joyful languages of song, colour and plenty. (It is
as Gerard Manley Hopkins' sonnet proclaims: every thing on earth
'finds tongue to fling out broad its name . . . *myself* it speaks and
spells' ('As kingfishers catch fire, dragonflies draw flame'; MacKenzie
1990: 141).) But, if this woman's husband feels anything, it is
apparently only vexation – or terror, terror of the elemental, of
expansive, passionate emotion and certainly of the speech that might
reveal it. So, instead of spontaneous self-expression, particularly in
response to another human being, this man prizes the rational dictates
of his 'wise ones': the considered, the conventional, the customary –
good form, good taste and good conduct. No wonder his wife's desire
is vexatious to him and his limitation a bore to her. Unable to talk with
her husband, her communication is restricted to the cold and silent
language of numbers in the tradesmen's accounts – and to prayer for
the end of her life.

But still, the woman has not given up. She continues loving, even
though the poem says it is a 'labour' that inspires nothing in return but
the provision of necessities and the dreary certainty of an 'orderly'
funeral when she is 'still'. And she does express herself, for she writes
her poem. Besides, its form, as well as its content, speaks out for the

'feminine'. It does so using language in ways which have been prized as female – but also mocked.

Take, to begin with, grammatical choices. Otto Jespersen, a Danish linguist writing in the first quarter of this century, believed women do not favour syntactic constructions which can signal relationships between ideas. That is, they avoid *hypotactic* constructions, clause sequences which are linked by subordinating conjunctions like *when*, *because* and so on. Instead, according to Jespersen, women choose *parataxis*, a string of independent main clauses, or else link these simply with co-ordinating conjunctions like *and* or *but*. In consequence, he argues, women may limit the cool expression of logical connections, and, in compensating for their deficiency – regrettably, he seems to imply – emphasize emotion instead. For, according to Jespersen, women use stress and intonation, instead of grammar, to mark the 'gradation between the respective ideas' (Jespersen 1922: 251). His disdain may seem odd, for once upon a time women were criticized not for excess but for lack of emotion! As Coates points out (1986: 28), Rousseau once found female writing pretty and witty, but cold, without soul. Yet the contradiction, Coates suggests, is explicable according to the 'Androcentric Rule': that is, whatever is male is found commendable but, in a woman, objectionable.

In fact Wickham uses (as does Swift in his poem) both sorts of syntactic construction throughout 'Nervous prostration', the admired hypotaxis as well as the disparaged parataxis and co-ordination. Line 3, for instance, is a sentence made up of two main clauses linked by *and*: lines 5–8 of the final stanza are an example of the 'Chinese box' arrangement of main and subordinate clauses so admired by Jespersen. In any case, the co-ordinating conjunctions slighted by Jespersen are far from impotent. The 'feminine' construction – resembling to Jespersen (charmingly, perhaps, but inadequately) 'a set of pearls joined together on a string of *ands* and similar words' (1922: 251) – is pefectly capable of expressing links, like those of cause and effect. For example, beginning the poem's second sentence with *and* coheres it with the first: vexation and boredom, hints 'And', may have a lot to do with marriage to a particular class of man. Later in the stanza, *so* makes clear the consequences of Croydon's limitations.

On the other hand, Wickham is certainly 'guilty' of using emotional intonational curves and stresses. These are not at all restrained, not even by the patterning force of regular metrical rhythm. Though one line of four main stresses is generally followed by one of three, in pairs throughout the poem, the lines vary considerably in numbers of syllables and secondary stresses. Moreover, the tone nuclei and stresses (see chapter 3) mark where the speaker's strongest feelings lie. They emphasize verbs – *say*, *sing*, *turn*, *live*, *love*, *speak* – all of them actions, communicative actions moreover, that the speaker desires her Croydon man to carry out. But she hopes in vain, and an arguably greater emphasis falls on the one and only significant 'action' her husband does accomplish – or, rather, by default causes to happen: he *bores* her. It remains only for her to stress, and to despair of, her own ineffectual activities – the vexing and the wishing – and to cry out the sobbing and the shrieking, those inarticulate, emotional activities with which this woman might hope to force life from the Croydon class.

Yet of course, whilst Jespersen might have winced, present-day feminists might applaud this expression of feeling. Recently women have insisted on the value of 'feminine' language use that emphasizes emotion and 'speaks' the body. For example, the French linguist, Julia Kristeva, argues that meaning can only be completely expressed 'if one plays on the whole register of language', if one uses all its resources including not only rhythm and intonation but also textual disruption, for she believes these give an 'inscription of that same emotion which transverses syntax but integrates the message' (in Moi 1986: 317; and see Cameron 1985 for a full discussion of feminist applications of linguistic theory by Kristeva, Irigaray and others).

One such textual disruption appears in Wickham's third stanza when the fourth line is interjected in apposition to the quoted speech of line 3. There is a different kind of subversion in the initial line of stanza 2 when its first two most naturally stressed syllables – 'green fields' – fall together and are not, as in other lines, separated by an unstressed syllable to match the expected metrical pattern. The established rhythm is thus broken – as well it might be, considering the poem's shift at this point from frustration and limitation to the unrestricted energy of the natural world.

But then, such emotional irregularity, as well as impassioned intonation and stress, are not enjoyed only by women. These aspects of language are available to both sexes, in everyday discourse as well as in art, and they are neither (depending on your point of view) purely a woman's privilege nor her particular weakness. Kristeva explains that in the young child, male and female, there exists what she calls the *semiotic* state. It is the forerunner of the rhythms, intonational flow and textual disruptions of adult speech but, says Kristeva, when symbolic language is acquired the semiotic is repressed. She therefore calls it 'feminine' – *not* because it is exclusive to women but because its use, by both men and women, may be undervalued and restricted, subjected to the kind of marginalization that women encounter. However, in some genres the semiotic is not so repressed. It is more in evidence in poetry – poetry written by men as well as by women (Hopkins has already been mentioned in this chapter and his Sprung Rhythm comes to mind). Yet, in Swift's 'The furniture of a woman's mind', it seems restricted beneath the inexorably smooth regularity of his confident jingle, the poem's lines generally end-stopped, its metrics neatly perfect.

And it is patriarchal arrogance of Swift's sort, expressed in a variety of ways, that recent studies in language and gender have found in the everyday language use of men, limiting and disadvantaging women. (These studies are discussed in detail in Coates 1986.)

For example, Zimmerman and West (1975) heard men interrupting women's talk far more than each other's – a liberty women did not take with male speech. And when men took the floor, Swacker (1975) found they exploded the myth of chattering women and more reflective men by sustaining lengthy monologues – and monologues of course invite only silence, not the linguistic responses that bring another speaker into conversation.

Still, these studies also suggest that women, like the poem's speaker, do want their men to 'turn and talk'. Fishman (1980) heard women asking men questions, and questions require answers. Moreover, once a reaction has been provoked, women are likely to keep their men talking with plenty of encouraging minimal responses, the *mhm*s, *right*s, *yes*es that indicate listeners are attending and interested to hear more.

However, in so doing women may facilitate their own repression, for in supporting the monologues that can overwhelm, these tactics may leave them only the options of silence – or the equally debilitating sobs and shrieks of 'nervous prostration'. And, if a woman does manage, against the odds, to take her conversational turn, men may, as Zimmerman and West observed, deny her the encouragement of minimal responses, the *mhm*s, *right*s and *yes*es.

Wickham's poem takes a turn of course. Its persona does manage to speak out, making statements, expressing a point of view. It is in fact a kind of monologue. Yet will it communicate, will it have the advantage, like its male counterparts, of being listened to and clearly heard? For poetry has no immediate or guaranteed audience. It is as solitary in its writing as the diary entry, and less sure of response than the letter, the two genres through which women have traditionally expressed themselves. So it is not surprising that Wickham's speaker still wishes, despite her art, that the 'gentleman', her very proper husband, might one day turn to her and talk.

Nevertheless, if the poem does reach an audience, it is certainly, as R.D. Smith suggests, introducing *The Writings of Anna Wickham, Free*

Woman and Poet (1984), 'good propaganda' in its representative image of silent man and silenced woman. Yet Smith feels 'Nervous prostration' is not Wickham's best work because, in his view, it is, 'at the last, unfair' (1984: 10). But unfair in what respect? It is certainly not unreasonable in the sense of total fabrication, for the poem seems to be to some extent autobiographical, its speaker to be modelled on Anna herself.

To begin with, Anna Wickham did indeed marry a 'man of the Croydon class': Patrick Hepburn, solicitor and astronomer. She – the daughter of intelligent, creative and sensitive parents – saw herself as lower middle class. But Patrick's family, she explains in her auto-biography (part of which is included, together with a selection of poems and other prose, in Smith 1984) lived in Croydon and were members of

> the upper middle-classes, the villa-dwellers who scorned my father for tuning their pianos and my mother for selling them their rotten waltzes in a shop. . . . I now realise that they [my parents] more than half admired the villa-dwellers for using and abusing their privilege, and were more than a little inclined to kiss the hand that struck them. But when I was a child, and too long into my womanhood, I believed in this class war.
>
> (1984: 83)

Furthermore, it really 'wasn't good form in the Croydon class / To say you love your wife'. At least, *en route* to meet his relations, Patrick urged Anna not to show him too much affection before his cousins (Smith 1984: 138). And the Hepburns' sense of order and taste – they could certainly be counted on to organize the orderly funerals and restrained mealtimes of the poem – was not Anna's. Patrick's step-mother's house, she wrote, 'was ugly, orderly and without taste. . . . Out of this house came gloom that could have been cut with a knife' (Smith 1984: 140).

As for mutual conversation, Patrick did 'turn and talk' – but at, rather than to, Anna. She found he 'needed an audience' and, enjoying what she called his lecturettes (reminiscent of the male monologues referred to above?) she provided a 'supremely good' one (Smith 1984: 129–30). But the arrangement was too one-sided for Anna and she declares, a few pages later in her autobiography, 'I needed to talk to Patrick as well as have him talk to me' (Smith 1984: 149).

She also needed him to *listen* to her talk, particularly to acknowledge her poetry. But Patrick forbade her to publish some of her poems. His behaviour was aggressive and, in resisting, Anna pushed her arm through a glass panel and cut her wrist. A doctor was called and Anna was certified and hospitalized, in a private asylum, for six weeks. So much for the poem's hope of 'sobs and shrieks' provoking a loving, speaking reaction.

Nevertheless, Smith explains that – in real life as well as in her poem – Anna persisted with her 'labour' of love: 'she always put them [her husband and children] first in her practical and moral priorities' (Smith 1984: 18).

Besides, both Smith and Wickham's son, James, believe there was more to Anna's love than labour. Smith thinks there was probably passion in the relationship as well as regard, whilst James has 'no doubt that Anna and Patrick loved each other' (Smith 1984: 17, xx). And as for the conflict, Smith explains that Anna herself displayed sado-masochistic symptoms, probably engendered by her own mother's 'often farouche behaviour . . . her sometimes savage discipline' (Smith 1984: 5). Moreover, for Smith, some of Anna's best work 'celebrates the violent struggles' (1984: 17) of her relationship with Patrick. Certainly the speaker in 'The tired woman', for example, urging her lover to 'blind' her, to 'bind' her with cords and to 'drive' her through 'a silent land / With the compelling of your open hand' (Smith 1984: 198) tells a very different story from 'Nervous prostration'. Perhaps then, in not making these complexities clear, the poem is, as Smith claims, unfair?

Moreover, references to the Croydon 'class' and to 'maxims their wise ones teach', do not make clear that women, as well as men, played a significant role in Anna's unhappy frustration. Yet, according to her autobiography, the Hepburn sisters were, in their stiff correctness, as much at fault as Patrick, perhaps more so.

> It had been the reinforcement of his hereditary characteristics by his sisters from Tonbridge and Bromley and Worthing that had spoiled my relationship with him. . . . They created an atmosphere in which my spirit could not keep alive; and I was avid to keep my spirit alive. If I could have got the clean but nauseating smell of these good women out of my nostrils, if I could have washed my nervous tissue clear of their obtrusions, my sense of humour, which was soon to revive, might have healed my relationship with my husband.
>
> (Smith 1984: 155–6)

It might have done. It is true that a sense of humour runs throughout Anna's autobiography. And perhaps wry descriptions, like her portrait of Aunt Florrie who 'dominated all her nephews and nieces by giving them presents of complicated electro-plate contrivances for warming the breakfast dishes, and dinner gongs of a standard pattern' (Smith

1984: 140), were a quiet way to some kind of sanity when the noisier sobbing and shrieking failed. This particular portrait's punch line – 'Wherever she planted a dinner gong she seemed to eliminate personality' – may, in its jokey hyperbole, trivialize and so neutralize any disturbing implications.

But perhaps a touch of the same mildly sarcastic jokiness in 'Nervous prostration' – present, for example, in its jaunty rhythm, and in the alliteration of 'Croydon class' – masks the complexities of Anna's life, suppressing the love, underestimating the power of the Hepburn women and producing as a result an oversimplified caricature of a situation, a simplification deserving Smith's criticism that it is 'strident' as well as unfair (1984: 10).

So laughter may not always be the best medicine. But then, if other strategies go unheard, its 'strident' (according to Smith) rhetoric can be the only remedy available. Besides, 'Nervous prostration' is hardly as blatant a cartoon of a private relationship as Jonathan Swift's image of massed, chattering women. Moreover, one poem cannot represent an entire life and its 'unfairness' may be remedied if it is read in company with other poems and Anna's prose writings.

Still, Smith's observations of unfairness and stridency are a reminder that not only those images of male/female language which (like Swift's poem) ridicule women, but also those that are sympathetic, are sometimes partial truths: they may be so of necessity, either for the sake of making a message heard, or because the complexity of that message defies complete description. However, if these images and arguments are taken to mean that women are *inevitably* disenabled by the language of men, they distort the situation in ways that can be unhelpful to the feminist cause.

For example, it would be unfair to assume, encouraged by the title of Dale Spender's *Man Made Language* (1980), and by some of its arguments based on the Sapir–Whorf hypothesis (discussed here in chapter 4), that men alone 'languaged' the world to their own satisfaction and to women's disadvantage – so that we 'can see only certain arbitrary things' (Spender 1980: 139). For it is disenabling and unrealistic, given the creative potential of language which is available to all human beings (see chapter 2), to assume that women can play no part in the naming of experience. Indeed, Spender herself acknowledges that women can see through the words and structures of patriarchal preference to choose fresh language to express their own particular perceptions. How else could she have issued her own challenge?

But the operative word here is 'choose'. Robin Hamilton's poem

'Semantic fairytale' (1985: 163) deals with the issue of language and perceptual choice through an adaptation of the Hanzel and Gretel fairytale. The two children are captured by a witch, Hanzel popped into an oven, Gretel trapped in a cage. For Hamilton, the oven and the cage are both, metaphorically, snares of language. That is, Hamilton images both genders (not merely the female) affected, in Sapir–Whorf fashion, by the shaping force of language – but both, despite the apparent constrictions and distortions of the language surrounding them, are content with their lot: 'Instead of escaping they came to love the words that lapped them.' Gretel's cage was a 'cage of Motherhood' but she repeated without question the words she had inherited, accepting without thought their traditional images of a woman's life. Chirruping in her cage she 'only wished to become a parrot'.

Of course, for many women motherhood and the family is *not* a trap. And not all men understand by 'motherhood' the kind of role which oppresses a woman. Yet, from a feminist perspective, the traditional and eulogized patterns of marriage and motherhood can be inhibiting and restricting to a woman, making her feel guilty if she does not match them to perfection whilst supporting the oppressive power of male partners and fathers. But it would seem that Gretel is not alone in accepting this kind of 'cage', in preference to making alternative language choices which would express and encourage a different perception of a woman's role – not if the stacks of women's magazines, telling in traditional words and syntax the tale of passive heroines still waiting for their prince to come, say anything about the real-life aspirations of their readers.

But whilst women might profitably change their language choices – insisting, for instance, that *he or she* replace the conventional, female-excluding *he* – it is surely misleading to assume, however correct Irigaray is about stultifying 'male' logic, that the very nature of language requires radical alteration to meet women's special needs. In fact, it could hardly be changed, since the elements and structures of human language appear to have an innate foundation (see chapter 2). Irigaray herself accepts that 'what a feminine syntax might be is not simple nor easy to state'. She suggests it would have neither subject nor object, and no proper names, involving instead 'nearness, proximity'. But it is hard to see any of this as 'language'. Indeed Irigaray herself, apparently describing a form of communication far more limited than language, says of her feminine 'syntax' that 'the place where it could best be deciphered is in the gestural code of women's bodies. . . . In suffering, but also in women's laughter' (Irigaray 1985: 134). So the pursuit of a completely different kind of communication is surely a fruitless exercise, distracting from the real issue – the way we choose to *use* the elements of language we presently have.

However, despite the immense value of emotional expression which feminist linguistics rightly emphasizes, it would surely be counter-productive to encourage a 'feminine' use which exclusively 'speaks the body' in *preference* to logic. For of course, as well as the communication of emotional meaning, the clarity and persuasiveness of structured argument is needed and, indeed, used by many women to effectively explain woman's point of view and to disentangle – querying the premises on which offending logic is based – its masculine distortions.

One of these premises, shared by men and women, is that men have power and women are powerless. But, whatever the social accuracy of this assessment, it is unfair, to both sexes, to assume that all women are, by definition, *linguistically* weak and all men are strong. However correct in their particular contexts those studies may be which show women struggling to make themselves heard in mixed-group discourse, there are other investigations which, in different countries, find the gender power balance equalled or reversed. This suggests that language power is partly a matter of situation, not simply of gender. For instance, O'Barr and Atkins (1980) found that in courtroom discourse women in powerful positions – those with high status in terms of job, education or expertise in relation to a trial – spoke 'powerfully', with confidence, whilst men in weaker positions, perhaps in low-status jobs or un-employed, used language less powerfully.

However, it is not possible to pinpoint forms of language which are *automatically* and consistently powerful. Their effect depends on the whole 'package' of language choices. For instance a *tag* question, such as *This is the right room* **isn't it?** 'tagged on' to the end of a remark, may seem to undercut the assurance of the statement to which it is attached. On the other hand, tags can be powerful, achieving an answer from a reluctant co-conversationalist. Or they can be facilitators, unaggressive but firmly drawing responses from the shy or nervous. Their weakness, or their strength, will be recognizable partly in their tone and partly from surrounding language use (also see Holmes 1984).

There is also power in less obviously 'strong' language. Take, for instance, gossip. Although Swift ridiculed scandal-mongering over morning tea, gossip is not always scurrilous and destructive – and it can be powerful in other ways. Emler argues that it is a complex and vital way of sifting the kind of information we need in order to function effectively in society (1990: 171–93). Hearing who is doing this or that – who is about to leave a job, a spouse, a house, what changes in work or community the grapevine predicts – helps us to decide our own moves. Nor is gossip a skill exclusive to women. It is a strength shared by both sexes but termed by men, according to Emler, 'talking politics'.

Still, the manner of women's gossiping may be different from men's, its intrinsic power augmented by co-operation rather than by self-assertion. Coates argues that in all-women groups

> the *way* women negotiate talk symbolises . . . mutual support and co-operation: conversationalists understand that they have rights as speakers and also duties as listeners; the joint working out of a group point of view takes precedence over individual assertions.
>
> (Coates and Cameron 1988: 120)

The existence of many all-female groups, dedicated to mutual encouragement, endorses the point.

On the other hand, readers may also be aware, from their own experience, of conversationalists in all-women groups who are far from mutually approving and supporting but, on the contrary, skilfully undercut and demoralize other group members. The question of language and gender is evidently enormously complex, and there is no space here to even being to consider the further complexities that undoubtedly exist in cultures very different from our own.

But the situation for women and communication is surely less bleak than either Swift's or Wickham's poem suggests. For one thing, the social context is steadily changing, becoming more hopeful for women whose voices, encouraged and publicized by the feminist movement, are gaining platforms and being heard. Indeed, however justified a complaint about her personal life Wickham's poem may be, outside her marriage she herself was not totally silenced, her words consistently trivialized in Swiftian fashion. On the contrary, her compulsive writing – ove fourteen hundred poems 'essential to her sanity' (Smith 1984: 23) – was heard. It achieved an international reputation and was extensively anthologized. Louis Undermeyer, the American man of letters, wrote in his introduction to a collection including 'Nervous prostration' that

> a small and widely-scattered group of women are taking stock of themselves – appraising their limitations, inventions and energies without a thought of man's contempt or condescension. . . . The most typical, and in many ways the best of these seekers and singers is Anna Wickham.
>
> (in Smith 1984: 21)[2]

Even so, there is still a considerable way to go. But, whatever the way forward, it is clearly not through partial descriptions of women's language, its supposed weaknesses or even its supposed strengths, nor simply through training in 'assertive' language behaviour. Since women's language is, potentially, as strong and as expressive as men's these are misleading and ill-considered red herrings – a Swiftian 'set of phrases learnt by rote'.

SUGGESTIONS FOR FURTHER WORK

1 Read Robin Hamilton's 'Semantic fairytale' (Hamilton 1985: 163) and critically consider and develop my interpretation of this poem (given above, pp. 128–9). It is true that Hamilton is not uncritical of Hanzel's use of language. But, otherwise, might the poem, in its choice of gaoler and its image of Gretel as parrot, have been approved by Swift and others disdainful of women's language?

2 Listen to mixed-group conversations, and also to single-sex groups, and note the use of any of the following language manoeuvres (most of which are referred to in the chapter above). In the mixed groups are any of them used only by the men involved, or only by the women? Are all of them used in the single-sex groups? What do you think, in either kind of group, are the effects of the language tactics used? Do you think their social contexts, particularly in terms of power balances, affect who uses the manoeuvres and also their consequences?

(a) interruptions;
(b) overlaps (i.e. just 'clipping' – and therefore, perhaps, a less invasive language use than interruption – the end of the previous speaker's utterance);
(c) monologues;
(d) tag questions;
(e) minimal responses (*mhm, right, go on*);
(f) hedges (e.g. *sort of, just, you know* – phrases which literally hedge around, and therefore perhaps reduce the authority of, statements);
(g) paratactic or hypotactic constructions;
(h) intonational emphasis.

8 The power of discourse
David Lodge's novel *Nice Work* and poetry by Tom Leonard

The first half of this chapter draws, for a theoretical perspective, on Norman Fairclough's Language and Power *(1989), which has as backdrop (Fairclough's word) work by the linguist Halliday, the semiotician Kress and social theorists including Althusser, Foucault, Bourdieu and Habermas. The second half of the chapter looks in a related way at Sandra Harris's work on courtroom discourse.*

And their judges spoke with one dialect,
but the condemned spoke with many voices.

And the prisons were full of many voices,
but never the dialect of the judges.

And the judges said:
      'No-one is above the Law.'
          (Leonard 1986)

Tom Leonard's poem refers directly to the legal system, and this chapter will be partly concerned with the language of the courts. However, the concept of language as 'law' operates in other spheres. That is, it may be argued that we ourselves are constructed, determined, controlled by language and that total freedom of speech is mythical. As Robyn Penrose, the feminist academic in David Lodge's *Nice Work*, remarks to a would-be lover,

When I was younger . . . I allowed myself to be constructed by the discourse of romantic love for a while. . . . We aren't unique individual essences existing prior to language'.
(Lodge 1989: 293; all subsequent page references are to this edition)

The invented Robyn, tutoring her imaginary students, echoes real-world theorists, like Foucault and Derrida, and insists there is no 'finite, unique soul or essence that constitutes a person's identity; there is only a subject position in an infinite web of discourses – the discourses of power, sex, family, science, religion, poetry, etc.' (40). If she is right, then people are like chameleons, changing linguistically in some relationship to context. For Robyn, in her fictional life, uses the term 'discourse' roughly as, for example, Fairclough does in reality (1989: 20–31), referring to language, both its production and its understanding, as social practice, a process that is a part of society, conditioned by its structures yet also contributing to the creation of those structures.

But of course, David Lodge is taking a humorous look at a serious proposition, one debated by theorists (including Lodge himself), and, I suggest, implied by Leonard's poem. *Nice Work's* polarization of views on the subject makes comical both the theorists and their arguments. Nevertheless, Lodge's witty exposure throws into explanatory relief aspects of language and of language use which, in the real world, may have a powerful and complex potential that is very far from comic. What follows shares the humour of the novel, but at the same time endorses the importance of the themes with which it plays.

FOR LOVE, LANGUAGE – OR MONEY?

In the imaginary world of Rummidge, Robyn Penrose's thesis, earnestly and endlessly argued, bemuses the strong and (at least in her presence) comparatively silent Vic Wilcox, Managing Director of Pringle's engineering firm (whom Robyn meets when she is required by her university to learn about his business through 'shadowing' him at work). In particular, Vic is horrified that Robyn sees love as essentially linguistic, for he is also her would-be suitor. Robyn herself would, presumably, have been amused by my choice of noun – 'suitor' – apparently straight from what she classes as the romantic kind of discourse, the kind of talk that, in her estimation, makes its users lovers of the soulful, dogged kind. But Vic is perfectly sure he is no mere 'subject position', shaped and varying only according to the language he uses, so that he is sometimes the lover, sometimes the manager, sometimes – placed by Robyn's own discourse as she, 'ever the teacher' (292), explains to him theories of semiotics, linguistics and the nineteenth-century novel – the compliant student. On the contrary, Vic, bewitched and bewildered, is convinced he is a unique 'self', a character, an identity, a person who enjoys passionate feelings for Robyn that, whatever she may think, are no 'bourgeois fallacy' (293), and definitely much more enjoyable than words and syntax.

But it is perhaps no wonder that Vic is puzzled by Robyn's theories of language. For one thing, as David Lodge's narrator sees it, Robyn's own behaviour is not noticeably affected by her academic arguments: 'she seems to have ordinary human feelings, ambitions, desires, to suffer anxieties, frustrations, fears, like anyone else in this imperfect world' (40–1). Besides, before meeting her and hearing her discuss Tennyson, the Brontës and George Eliot, the only manifestations of language of which Vic had been hyper-conscious were the syrupy lyrics of popular songs, particularly those of Jennifer Rush.

Robyn would probably call these songs *texts*, a term used by linguists and semioticians for any spoken or written product of underlying discourses – in this case, the discourse of romance. But, immersed in Rush's words of 'heart' and 'warmth' and 'tenderness', as they ooze seductively out of his car radio, nothing so technical occurs to Vic, dreaming his way across Rummidge from home, to factory, to Robyn's university room. It certainly never crosses his mind that the singer's language – anyone's language – might be as Robyn insists: a 'devious and slippery medium' (340). On the contrary: aware that his body and his emotions are perceptibly aroused, he finds puzzling, to say the least, Robyn's view that love is merely 'a literary con-trick . . . an advertising con-trick . . . a media con-trick'. He quite definitely cannot agree that there is nothing outside language. '"I don't accept that", he said, lifting his chin and locking his gaze on hers. "It would mean we have no free will"' (362).

Yet Robyn insists Vic has misunderstood the subtleties of her thesis. After all, she did explain to him that she had 'allowed' (293) herself to be constructed by the language of love, and her selection of verb, *allowed*, does suggest a degree of choice and autonomy in the matter. Besides, she argues patiently, once the subject accepts that there is nothing much to life outside of language s/he can begin to write his/her own script!

This mix of determinism and creativity, argued by Robyn in her lecture theatre and displayed in her bedroom, is one that Fairclough discusses with regard to the world outside the pages of novels. He explains the argument (1989: 92) that many discourses have become *naturalized*, so accepted that, as they manifest themselves in texts, the ideologies they carry – the dominant ideologies of the powerful – are consented to by the less powerful, without coercion, as if they were '*common sense*'. Discourses are, then, both products and preservers of existing social structures, the status quo. On the other hand, Fairclough explains, they can be not only the product of social structures but also their *producers*. That is, such 'reproduction', as Fairclough terms the process, 'may be basically conservative, sustaining continuity, or basically transformatory, effecting changes . . . structures may be produced anew with virtually no change, or . . . they may be produced anew in modified forms' (1989: 39).

So, as Robyn adopts discourse in which she is tutor to her hearers' subject position as students, she perpetuates (if, sometimes, in comically larger-than-real-life fashion) a conventional form of educational discourse, a traditional kind of teaching, a social structure which exists in the reality beyond Rummidge. But discourses and structures may be modified by their combination with other discourses resulting, as Fairclough explains, in a creativity of 'extension-through-combination' (1989: 31). And Robyn herself, in speaking with her students, does appear to combine the taken-for-granted discourse of teacher authority with a different kind of language.

Take, for example, some of the 'texts' constructed by Robyn and her student Marion Russell (with, and without, other students present). There is, for instance, Marion's request for a coursework extension (67–8), her tutorial and its intervening moments in the staff women's lavatory (334–9), and a discussion about Robyn's future plans (382–3).

All these have a 'naturalness' in Fairclough's sense of the word. He identifies (1989: 46) three typical aspects of any discourse which, when analysed, describe its essential quality: its *contents*, its *relations* and its *subjects*. In each of these respects Robyn behaves linguistically true to both Rummidge's and the real world's conventional ('common sense') lecturer form.

For, in the session designated as tutorial, she delivers her part of its expected *contents* – literary topics – in ways which establish her in an authoritative, professional *relationship* with a rather dependent group and place her in the *subject* position of tutor to the rest as students. That is, she talks '*patiently*' (338) and her syntactic forms are generally characterized by statements of *academic information* which are clear and comprehensive – so much so that her listeners can be certain she knows the answers to her occasional *open questions* and therefore assume these are merely posed to facilitate academic discussion (336–9). Then again, when Marion requests a coursework extension (67–8) Robyn makes further statements, one of *institutional regulations* and one *granting permission*.

All in all, then, these texts draw on conventional lecturer discourse. Contents, relations and subjects maintain Robyn's conventional professional role and Marion's relative position as dependent and learner. However, Robyn's talk with Marion is also somewhat personal – and is so in a way that suggests some creativity in her discourse.

For example, the incident when Robyn discovers Marion hiding in the staff women's lavatory, prior to the tutorial (334–9), appears in some way innovative. For the personal nature of Robyn's questions – 'What's the matter, Marion?. . . Pre-menstrual tension?', and the later 'Why not?' (i.e., why can Marion not join the tutorial?) – hint at a closer relationship than has, I think, always been usual between lecturers and students.

Of course, lecturer talk has traditionally included not only the language of pedagogy but also that of pastoral care. 'What is the matter?' may sound like a standard part of this interested, protective discourse transported into fiction. Yet Robyn seems to bring a relatively new dimension to a conventional blend. Her query, 'Pre-menstrual tension?' suggests the kind of shared female knowledge that can, in real exchanges as well as Lodge's fictional ones, mark discourse between women who are personally close – and equal – either as relations, friends or, maybe, sisters by right of feminism. And although Robyn and Marion are not related, are not friends outside the university, there is, as Robyn probes areas of the young woman's life beyond the campus, a suggestion in their discourse not simply of closeness but of the parity that is supposed to mark feminist sisterhood. Marian's giggly manner when she answers Robyn's queries about her modelling reinforces these indications and there is a further mark of egalitarianism when Marian chooses the staff, rather than the student, lavatory in which to hide. Robyn is evidently not surprised to find her there.

So here, in these texts and contexts – the traditional mix of teacher/carer blended with a more intimate and equal kind of talk and behaviour – we seem to have hints of that 'extension-through-combination' described by Fairclough, the creative 'reproduction' of a discourse type through meshed combinations.

Of course, intimate, sisterly discourse existed between unrelated women long before feminism acquired its name and its political edge. But for how long has it been combined with pedagogical discourse? Long enough in her fictional world, apparently, for Marian to accept it as if it were quite natural. She is perfectly prepared to talk to Robyn about her off-campus activities.

However, she is astonished when her tutor – apparently believing that she and Marion are, as young women, similarly exploited and oppressed – physically increases their linguistically created familiarity by sweeping the student into her arms (68). Sisterly behaviour of this warmth is evidently unusually close.

But Marian does not seem to resist. And acquiescence is hardly surprising. After all, however close her discourse and behaviour, Robyn is not Marian's 'equal' sister, but a powerful participant – *the* powerful participant – in their exchanges. As Lodge's narrator remarks 'Robyn tends to identify with the students against the system that assesses them, even though she is *part of the system*' (italics mine). That is, she may identify and so use a discourse of some parity, but still she remains controller.

Turning again from imaginary to actual academics and their work, Fairclough explains:

> The relations of power which obtain between social forces, and the way in which these relations develop in the course of social struggle, are the key determinant of the conservative or transformatory nature of reproduction in discourse. . . . If there is a shift in power relations through social struggle, one can expect transformation of orders of discourse . . . [but] even if power relations remain relatively stable, they need to renew themselves in a constantly changing world, and transformations of orders of discourse may thus be necessary even for a dominant social grouping to keep its position.
>
> (1989: 40)

Robyn is taking full account of a changing world, at least in the academic sphere, but she is not relinquishing her authority. Even whilst (prior to the tutorial) concerned about her student's health, she maintains her authoritative relationship and her subject position as lecturer. The question about Marion's menstrual cycle, for instance, is put 'briskly', as tutor to student (335): it expects an answer as of right. And, though Marion does respond elsewhere to Robyn's queries about her job (67–8), she delivers her answers with lowered eyes and a blush that gives them the flavour of a confession to a superior rather than of a shared confidence. There is no struggle, of the kind referred to by Fairclough, which results in a change of discourse for Robyn and Marian. There is only Robyn's choice – and she chooses to take command, as usual and without effort. True, it is Marian who selects the staff lavatory, in which one of their talks takes place, and her unconventional choice could suggest a challenge to the conventional hierarchy. However, it is more likely that, encouraged by Robyn's friendliness, she feels *permitted* to be there.

Overall, then, theirs is not a meeting of equals. It is hardly likely that Marian's language, as student, would address demanding personal queries to her tutor about, for example, her menstrual cycle. Certainly when, presumably encouraged by Robyn's familiarity, she asks her tutor about her future plans she is given short shrift, told these are 'a private matter', and she feels it necessary to apologize for rudeness (382).

In fact, a discourse strain of Robyn's extended-through-combination kind could, ironically, *increase* tutor control. For it seems to me that the intimacy which marks Robyn's exchanges with Marion, though a near relation of feminist discourse with its emphasis upon the solidarity of shared experience and knowledge, could, *because* it is blended with the conventional discourse of pedagogy, lose the equality and mutual support that are supposed to mark this kind of women's language and instead to border on the intrusive.

Real-world lecturers' discourse may also be mutating, taking account of developing social movements that include feminism. But is it, like Robyn's, easily maintaining authority? (See question 2 at the end of this chapter.)

In other respects, apart from Robyn's encounters with her students, *Nice Work* does demonstrate struggle. But even where there is tension, the dominant social structures (represented sometimes by individuals and sometimes by institutions) generally, as in Robyn and Marion's case, keep their position.

This may be seen in the clash between institutions: Rummidge University and the government. Rummidge tries to resist government economy-driven demands which, in effect, require it to adapt its discourse of collegiate institution to that of business. But, eventually, the university finds itself forced to recognize an educational con-sumerism and talk in terms of economies and enterprise (344). The actuality of redundancy – an economic reality like that of profit, loss and strike at Pringles – sees to it that the head of department starts reading the business pages of the *Guardian*, buys British Telecom shares and argues for 'cuts', cuts in syllabus and in staff (326, 344, 348–9). The once alien discourse of business finally prevails for Philip Swallow and his colleagues because matters outside of language insist that it does.

Of course there is constant struggle between Vic and Robyn, their opposite perspectives and their discourses inevitably thrown together by the Shadow Scheme. Sometimes their conflict does result in minor transformations. Vic's modified ways of thinking lead him to take down the pin-ups from Pringle and Sons' walls. As for Robyn, her father hears a new 'utilitarian' strain in her conversation and she herself is aware that she has adopted some of Vic's language, blending its economic arguments with her own concepts of equality of opportunity (307) – so much so that she willingly lends Vic money to start up a new business.

Usually, however, the status quo wins, the outcome of the struggle generally determined by the established power of the site in which it is conducted. Outside the factory and particularly in matters of love Robyn starts and finishes the relationship dominant, both linguistically, with her scoffing at romantic discourse, and physically since, when she goes to bed with Vic, she prefers 'to be on top' (293). But at the engineering works Robyn is on Vic's territory, and her academic discourse, with its ideologies of the evils of unemployment and inequality, are weak in the face of arguments for 'efficiency', 'competition', 'modernisation', 'redundancy' and 'rationalisation'. In consequence she is, for once in her life, especially given her sense impressions of a grim, dirty, noisy reality, literally 'lost for words' (120). When she does find her voice and warns a machine operative that he may lose his job, her language, stemming from a discourse alien to Vic's management ideologies, leads to a strike – a strike which, to her chagrin, threatens to lose the factory money and, consequently, the 'oppressed' workforce its jobs. As for Vic, his removal of the pin-ups is a factor in his eventual dismissal. For his behaviour appears to his colleagues 'a bit . . . eccentric' (385). And his superiors have, literally, the last word: they 'rationalise' him, true to their style of management, its discourse and its 'common sense' cutting of costs and personnel (a procedure whose profitability Vic himself endorsed and had only recently explained to Robyn and her colleagues (364)). As Fairclough explains:

> Individual creativity, in discourse and more generally, is never the wilful and extra-social business it is commonly portrayed as being: there are always particular social circumstances which enable it, and constrain it.
>
> (1989: 196)

Still – despite Vic's keen awareness that without financial backing he cannot begin again, and despite Robyn's theories of language's shaping power – the roots of the Wilcoxes' pleasure in each other as they plan their new business venture, and also of Robyn's desire to go on teaching regardless of her windfall, appear to lie outside economic and social circumstances, and outside language. They seem instead – as Vic would no doubt be happy to confirm – to some degree dependent upon these people as *individuals*.

Even so, it is no doubt the power of discourses, products and producers of social structures, which – as Robyn watches students and gardener instinctively inhabiting separate spheres in the university grounds – are seeing to it that there is 'a long way to go' (384) before the Utopian dream she entertains may be realized, of barriers coming down between social groups and of power being redistributed.

Which returns me from Lodge's novel to Tom Leonard's poetry and to the asymmetry of those who judge and those who are judged.

'AND THEIR JUDGES SPOKE WITH ONE DIALECT'

Leonard's reference to 'dialect' may be taken at face value. His judges apparently speak in a particular variety, or dialect, of their language and it is safe to assume that its accent, lexicon and syntax are those which mark the Standard version with its RP tones, that variety of English which (see chapter 6) can unite and symbolize the prestigious and the powerful. In this respect – since judges and magistrates are generally drawn from the middle class and upwards, with language to match – the poem is an accurate reflection of reality.[1] Leonard's poem further implies that, by contrast, those imprisoned (by these Standard speakers) use a *Non-standard* version of the language, versions of which there are as many as there are regions and which are generally assumed to be (and frequently are) markers of a lower class. Well, in truth, there are probably more working-class prisoners than there are middle and upper.

But the different 'voices' to which Leonard refers might just as well be different discourses. And here it is the discourse of the judges which prevails. Their discourse is as 'standard' as their accent: it is the law. No one may be above this law in the sense that no one, despite their inclination to different voices, is supposed to create their own alternative language, for no one can be above the judges, who (in their subject position of power and authority in relation to the subordinate roles of those who are witness or accused) approve and transmit its standard discourse.

And Leonard's poem is evidently representative of reality in this respect too. The ideology carried by the standard discourse of law, through the documents, reports, and courtroom exchanges that are its 'texts', includes, as Sandra Harris (forthcoming) points out, significant concepts like those of 'reason', 'justice' and 'legal rights and obligations'. Moreover, these concepts are understood in specific ways – those defined by the institution, perpetuated by its representatives (the 'court', the 'Bench') and generally accepted by all participants, powerful and powerless, as the kind of 'common sense' discussed earlier. Such abstracts may, it is true, be questioned, by drawing together disparate, contradictory discourses (rather as Fairclough's 'extension-through-combination' mentioned above) but, according to Kress (1985), they remain relatively fixed and stable.

Nevertheless, many solicitors and magistrates are aware of their linguistic power and point out that they believe themselves, through their language, to be taking care of defendants and clients. However, many of the papers written by members of the legal profession concentrate on the *clarity* of its language and on efforts to avoid jargon.

This is undoubtedly a step in the right direction, but Sandra Harris's work on the language of the courts (including 1984, 1988, 1989) finds limitation is particularly identifiable in the *interactive uses* to which language is put in the courtroom. The law's institutional limitation on creativity is demonstrated in her studies in the Arrears and Main-tenance sections of British Magistrates Courts. Here 'defendants speak for themselves directly to magistrates without the intervention or mediation of lawyers or other professionals . . . in a context where mainly middle-class magistrates and clerks interact with defendants who are predominantly working class or unemployed' (Harris forth-coming; other papers on courtroom discourse include Harris 1984, 1988, 1989).

Now, Grice has described interactive conversational practice as essentially *co-operative*, based on the observance of certain 'maxims' (1975: 45–6). He identifies these as the maxims of *quantity* (make your contribution no more nor less informative than necessary), *quality* (do not say that which you believe to be false or for which you have inadequate evidence), *relation* (be relevant) and *manner* (avoid obscurity and ambiguity and be brief and orderly). But, how-ever natural these maxims may be to ideal exchanges between equal conversationalists, Harris argues (ms.) that such co-operation is unlikely to be the underlying principle in a context where the goals of participants are, virtually by definition, in conflict. Her work demon-strates what might be called the – naturally – '*un*co-operative' language of those in authority, inhibiting the discourse of the rela-tively powerless.

She points out that Habermas, the social theorist, sees inequality of expression as a distortion of communication. However, speakers may accept such distortion as (in Habermas's terms) 'valid' if it appears to have a 'rightness' based on normative social rules. It may do so in what he calls *strategic* rather than *communicative* discourse (1984: 285–6): that is, discourse in which participants have, *normally*, asymmetrical access to the power of speech acts. The voices of the judged are never those of the judges. . .

Take, for example, the posing of questions, the prototypical court-room speech act. At least, it is the prototypical norm for 'repre-sentatives of the law': as one magistrate in Harris's data said to a defendant, 'I'm not here to answer questions – you answer *my* question' (forthcoming). Moreover, these interrogatives may be posed in such a way that their respondent is disadvantaged. That is, they may have a *presupposition* embedded in their syntax which the questioner may not be called upon to substantiate since, whilst the respondent is required to 'tell the truth, the *whole* truth and nothing but the truth', the questioner is not so obviously bound by Grice's maxim of quantity. Harris recorded, for instance, a defendant being asked 'Who wrote this letter for you?', a query which presupposes that *someone*, not the defendant, did the writing. The truth of such assumptions could be challenged of course but, in Harris's observations, it rarely was. Well, as Leonard's judge remarks, 'no-one is above the Law', and the defendant cannot easily, given the norms of the court, refute the 'validity' of the truths its representatives imply.

Besides, questions are specially difficult to challenge if they follow a 'narrative', told by a representative of the court and confirmed by the defendant. Harris (ms.: 15–16) heard a defendant agree with the clerk of the court that he had appeared before the court on an earlier date, had been fined a particular amount, had been ordered to pay it in instalments and had actually paid a certain sum. Immediately follow-ing this exchange the clerk posed a question asking the defendant to explain why he had 'chosen to ignore the order of the Court'. The defendant did not query the assumption that he *had* 'ignored' the order (though he might, on the contrary, have taken full account of it, yet been unable or unwilling to meet it) and instead, in answering the question, tacitly accepted it as if it had the same truth value as the rest of the narrative.

Moreover, a question such as this has the force of a secondary, potential function of interrogatives – that of accusation. Harris describes (ms.: 8) a series of questions posed by a magistrate to a defendant (who is requesting time to pay fines) about why the defendant has suddenly acquired money, how much money he is carrying and how he got to the court. The implication appears to be an accusation that he is using his money for purposes other than his fines. A direct accusation, 'You are squandering your money', could have been dealt with, denied or accepted, much more easily than one 'buried', as this is, in a question.

But, in any case, it is rare for a defendant to openly criticize the justice of the court. After all, to do so would be to challenge the accepted, ideologically weighted 'common sense' belief that courts are fair and no one is above their law. When, unusually, Harris did observe a defendant insisting 'I was totally unfairly judged to be guilty', she heard the magistrate deflect the challenge, rather than respond to it with consideration (forthcoming). He did so in a number of ways including stating that the case could not be retried, calling the imposed fine a 'debt' to be discharged rather than using the defendant's label of an 'injustice', and issuing a threat of prison if this fine was not paid.

Discourse analysis of this kind thus demonstrates and critiques the power and potential of language. But, in general, linguistics' own discourse has tended to endorse asymmetry. It has done so, Harris points out (ms.: 16–18), with its concepts of 'appropriacy' and 'competency', its notion that, *ideally*, language is matched to contexts by its users in ways that are 'appropriate' to the norms of those contexts. Such conformist users are assumed to have 'communicative competence'.

Yet the judges of so-called competency – 'judges' in and out of the law courts – are institutions and individuals with the power to define its norms and the discourses which maintain them. However much it may be desired, alternative, non-conformist communication is difficult in the face of its condemnation as abnormal and incompetent for the relatively powerless to justify, demonstrate – even to conceive. Of course, it is true that language is not without creative power. And through its users it does sometimes contribute, as Fairclough explains and as Lodge's Vic and Robyn demonstrate, to the shaping of new structures through the fresh combinations of discourses. Moreover, it can draw attention to asymmetry, as it does in the carefully chosen words of Leonard's poetry, and of Lodge's satire. Nevertheless, there are some voices which, stronger than others, carry further. Their word is law.

And the prisons were full of many voices
but never the dialect of the judges.

SUGGESTIONS FOR FURTHER WORK

1 There is a chapter in *Nice Work* (177–88) which begins with Robyn talking to her boyfriend Charles and goes on to a conversation between these two and Robyn's brother and his girlfriend. Charles eventually accuses Robyn of behaving patronizingly towards the other pair. 'Well, what can you talk about to people like that', asks Robyn defensively, no doubt implying that the four do not define 'nice work' in the same terms. How does each individual's language reveal and explain contrasting attitudes to their professional and personal lives?

2.

(a) The chapter has suggested, in its discussion of *Nice Work*, that real-world lecturers' discourse may be mutating, just as Robyn Penrose's appears to be changing in the fictional. Do readers, students or lecturers, find this to be true in their own experience? If so, in what ways?

(b) Further, are lecturers, whether or not their discourse is altering, maintaining power and authority (like Robyn)?

(c) Also, are there significant changes in student discourse, changes which increase student power? For instance, are students' relationships and subject positions altering (on staff–student consultative committees, perhaps)? Are there any new strains in their discourses? For example, is the language of economics, or perhaps a language of rights, obligations and law, entering student discourse with regard to course content, teaching and assessment?

9   The signalling of meaning
'Something for the time being' by Nadine Gordimer

Nadine Gordimer's short story, 'Something for the time being' (1983: 217–28), is discussed as a demonstration and interpretation of the signalling of meanings – meanings produced and constrained in relation to social power and solidarity – through a mixture of visual and behavioural signifiers as well as through language. Work by Peirce, Saussure and Barthes is referred to. Readers wishing to extend the discussion and to set it in a theoretical framework might see, for example, Introduction to Communication Studies *(Fiske 1982) and* Social Semiotics *(Hodge and Kress 1988).*

'Something for the time being' (Gordimer 1983: 217–28) is a short story about relationships in South Africa in the 1950s. A black husband, Daniel, is just out of jail, where he had been awaiting trial in a political case. Now, returned home to his wife, Daniel has lost his old job and is looking for a new one. A white husband, William, and his wife are concerned to provide work for Daniel, but William, a factory owner, will not allow Daniel to wear an ANC badge in the workplace. Daniel refuses to remove his badge and, in consequence, loses the job.

These are the bare bones of Nadine Gordimer's story, but the narrative's opening words concerning the black couple, 'He thought of it as discussing things with her', are the first of many indications that 'Something for the time being' is also about the processes of human communication. It is about success and failure in the signalling and discovering of meaning, so that Madge Chadders eventually declares of her husband, William, 'I'm beginning to get to know you', and Daniel comes to believe that his wife, Ella, has at last revealed to him hostile attitudes she has held, undeclared, for years. But, are Madge and Daniel correct in their understanding of their partners' meanings? And are they themselves able to make their own meanings clear to William and Ella? In considering questions of this kind the chapter draws together

Literature about Language's two central themes: (a) the immense power of language and (b) constraints upon that power.

The chapter is divided into four sections. The first describes some of the different signs of meaning available to us and exemplifies these through 'Something for the time being'. The second section considers the evaluation of signs of meaning, particularly through narrative form (a subject referred to in chapter 1 and developed in chapter 5). The third section discusses William, Daniel, Madge and Ella's signficantly different responses to two particular signs in their story and considers possible reasons for these differences. Finally, the fourth section extends this discussion of different responses and of factors, outside language and other sign systems, that can shape our reactions to communication.

SIGNS AND THEIR UNDERSTANDING

'Something for the time being' is partly about communication through the largely *arbitrary symbols* of the spoken word. The notion of arbitrariness was mentioned in chapter 1, explaining that, as a rule, words are arbitrary in the sense that they bear no resemblance to their referents. An exception would be onomatopoeic words.

Daniel's second name is apparently an arbitrary symbol of a particular kind. It is arbitrary because there is no clear relationship between it and Daniel's person, so much so that William Chadders has no clue to decide whether the man is called 'Mongoma' or 'Ngoma' or merely 'something like that'. Because a majority of language symbols – not merely the obvious example of proper names – are arbitrary in a similar way, it is their users who assign meanings to them, meanings that are generally agreed upon, as a rule or convention, by their speech community. Names are thus invested with what is known of their owners' identities. Of course, the meanings of names will be understood by a much more limited set of users than the meanings of common nouns which are shared by a whole community. For whilst 'Mongoma' (or 'Ngoma'), with regard to Daniel, indicates the particular set of meanings a particular user associates with him, it is likely to carry different implications in relation to another person of that name and, indeed, when used by a different person who knows Daniel in a different way. (For a discussion of proper names in communication see Marmaridou 1989.) But, in this case, William cannot be sure of any name at all and Madge is irritated, no doubt because her husband's uncertainty appears to signal his limited recognition or personal knowledge of Daniel as an individual.

When symbols are arbitrary it is – as the Swiss linguist, Ferdinand de Saussure pointed out – nothing inherent within them but their *difference*, one from another, that signals a difference of meaning. He told his students (who published notes from his lectures in 1915 after his death), 'in language there are only differences without positive terms' (1966: 115). That is, the phoneme /k/ is not /h/ because it sounds different: *cat* is not *hat* not only because it sounds different but also because *cat*, unlike *hat*, is not inanimate, or worn on the head, and so on. Gordimer's short story foregrounds this principle, for one of its major themes is expressed by contrastive selections from the following set, or paradigm, of nouns. The set is a 'paradigm' because all the words in it are related, in this case by the morpheme *thing*, but each is distinguishable from the rest by its particular prefix.

something
everything
anything
nothing

Daniel, Ella remembered from their courting days, did not want 'something for himself, like other young men she knew, but everything, and for *the people*'. Madge, on the other hand, always preferred to do 'something', believing (as she did in the case of Daniel's cleaning job and of her own varied efforts against apartheid) 'anything is better than nothing'.

But 'Something for the time being' is not only in and about significantly different arbitrary symbols. In addition it is about *metaphors*, like the 'black bird', that dangerous statement ('I'm not angry. I'm beginning to get to know you') released from Madge's lips before she fully understands its significance. And metaphor, of course, exploits *similarity* more than difference, signifying meaning by drawing attention to certain properties that entities have in common. The story is also about non-arbitrary indicators of meaning, *icons* and *indexes*, not only in language but also in objects, visual images, body language and so on. Above all, it is about all these signifiers in *interactional use*.

The philosopher C.S. Peirce (collected works 1931–58) described categories of signs and included symbols, icons and indexes in his classification. Icons resemble that to which they refer. A zig-zag road sign, for instance, warns of a zig-zag bend. In spoken language, onomatopoeic sounds are iconic in their similarity with their referent. In 'Something for the time being' Daniel's ANC badge has on it an outline of Africa: the sign is iconic in that it roughly matches the continent's shape. An index, on the other hand, is based on contiguity or causality, in the way that spots indicate measles and a spontaneous shriek can sound distress. Home, after the theatre, Madge's 'gasps and groans' are indexical of her 'pleasure at the release from the pressures of company noise'. Later, her repeated smoothing of her nightgown over the shape of her knees also seems an indexical sign, neither arbitrary nor iconic, but a reaction connected with her feelings, feelings of confusion and belligerence as she tries to make comfortable sense of her husband's behaviour in forbidding a man to wear his ANC badge.

However, signs are not always of one pure kind or another but may convey meaning in a number of simultaneous ways. For example, Daniel's thin suit has iconic significance when he is wearing it with 'a sharp-brimmed grey hat tilted back on his small head', for then he looks '*rather like* one of those boy-men who sing and shake before a microphone, and whose clothes admirers try to touch as a talisman' (italics mine). But the choice of clothing and its style of wearing might also seem, to admirers, an index of something special in Daniel's essential self, an index so potent that the clothes, like those of pop stars, become a magic charm.

Nevertheless, the phrase 'boy-men' could suggest – its qualification of 'men' with 'boy' seems to me mildly disparaging – that not every observer is an admirer. Indeed, the story makes clear that the construction and comprehension of signals is rarely a simple matter that produces a dictionary of signs related unambiguously to their referents. On the contrary, signs in *use* are shaped – and confused – by contextual, social factors, factors that include the asymmetries of power existing between participants in communication.

For instance, Daniel's old employers were Jews. Their Jewishness is signalled in their accent, the kind of marker that Hodge and Kress (1988: 76–86) call a *metasign*, a broad indication, like the lexical and syntactic distinctions of dialects, of social allegiance and shared culture. But, to Daniel, in the privacy and security of his own home, Mr Solly's voice 'suddenly presented . . . the irresistibly vulnerable' and, mimicking it – 'Ve vant to give you a tsance, but you von't let us' – he can take over and mock, 'half angry, resentfully amused', this sign of his former boss's identity. The mimicry turns an indication of solidarity into one of mild antagonism towards the employer who had always, until this occasion, kept work for Daniel through his spells in jail.

Then again, *outside* his workplace, William Chadders may sympathetically accept the drawing on Daniel's ANC badge as an icon of Africa, and the wearing of the badge as an index of a political position that Chadders understands; but, *inside* the workplace, it is unacceptable. In Sausssurian terms the drawing is a *signifier*, its *signified* the mental image of Africa that is experienced by those who see it, the *sign* these two in meaningful combination. But this sign is itself a signifier in what the French theorist, Roland Barthes, writing about 'semiotics' or the science of signs, called a 'second-order semiological system' (1973). For whilst it means, firstly, 'Africa, the continent', it can then, secondly, carry for those who wear it 'myths', stemming from the ideologies they share. In this usage 'myth' does not, of course, mean falsehood. It implies a particular way of understanding, not necessarily consciously realized – and whilst everyone seeing the badge is likely to agree the map on it means Africa, not everyone will have in mind the same second-order myth. Differences of culture, social or political background, individual experience and personality can affect its communication of meaning and cause misunderstanding as well as understanding.

However, it is because William Chadders does share some of Daniel's ideas and beliefs, signed by the badge, that he would not object to its wearing beyond the factory gates. Even so, *inside* the workplace the button's political implications are unacceptable to Chadders, for worn here it is an index of a dissatisfaction (connected with those who, in effect, do not share the same myth) that is at odds with the relative contentment of the factory's stable workforce, a black labour force that Chadders has managed to employ 'in this crazy country . . . with better working conditions than most'.

Hodge and Kress explain discrepancies of this kind as a consequence of a *logonomic system*.

> a set of rules prescribing the conditions for production and reception of meanings; which specify who can claim to initiate (produce, communicate) or know (receive, understand) meanings about what topics under what circumstances and with what modalities (how, when, why). . . . The logonomic rules are specifically taught and policed by concrete social agents (parents, teachers, employers) coercing concrete individuals in specific situations by processes which are in principle open to study and analysis. . . . Logonomic systems cannot be invisible or obscure, or they would not work. They become highly visible in politeness conventions, etiquette, industrial relations, legislation, and so on.
>
> (Hodge and Kress 1984: 4)

Such systems can, however, as Hodge and Kress point out, be resisted. For example, Flora Donaldson, who organized help for political prisoners, apparently did not respond as might be expected to the usual rules, for she 'looked just like any white woman who would automatically send a black face round to the back door, but she didn't seem to know that she was white and you were black'.

So, given all this diversity and complexity of signing, and of mixed responses to signifiers, how might readers make sense of signs of meanings as they appear in a short story?

THE MEANINGS OF NARRATIVE

It would appear that narrative structuring is acquired at a very young age (Mandler 1984: 50–3; Mancuso 1986: 91–110) and by widely diverse cultures. There are culture-specific differences (see, for example, Maranda and Maranda 1970, and Sutton-Smith 1986: 67–90) but, generally speaking, we appear to use the story, as discussed in chapters 1 and 5, as heuristic device, a way of making sense of our experiences – of deciding what they mean to us.

Labov has described (as discussed in chapters 1 and 5) a model of personal narratives, the kind of stories that we exchange constantly in informal conversation as a descriptive and explanatory device, detailing and assessing the events of our lives. Such narratives may include a number of components but essentially they are based upon what Labov calls the 'complication', sentences referring to the chronological events of a tale: this happened, and then that, and finally this. If the complication is reorganized we are telling a different tale or else nonsense: 'He came. He saw. He conquered' is a different tale from 'He conquered. He came. He saw.' But a sophisticated story goes beyond complication to 'evaluation', assessing what events meant to participants at the time of their occurrence and/or, what they mean now to the story-teller. Evaluation can be overt:

Julius Caesar came and investigated. *Liking* what he saw, he set out to conquer – *which wasn't good news for the locals.*

But it can also be built in to every choice and arrangement of language made in the telling of the story. Even the brevity and simplicity of the three original sentences in the Caesar narrative may carry a kind of message – perhaps an indication of the confidence, swiftness and sureness with which, in the narrator's view, the take-over took place. (Also see Biber and Finegan 1989 for a discussion of what they call 'stance', the expression of attitudes, feelings and judgements in language.)

Literary narratives, by definition, include the complication. Their evaluation can take a variety of forms, much of it subtly embedded in phonological, lexical and syntactic choices. For instance, when Daniel is described as looking, in his suit and hat, like one of those 'boy-men', the pop-stars 'whose clothes admirers try to touch as a talisman', it seems to be (as mentioned earlier) that mild disparagement is signalled in the qualification of 'men' with 'boy'.

` However, a considerable part of evaluation in 'Something for the time being' is of the overt kind, in the form of a narrating voice interpreting the communicative acts of the story's protagonists and other signs of meaning in their environments. For example, the story's introductory sentence. 'He thought of it as discussing things with her', is completed with the words, 'but the truth was that she did not help him out at all' – the 'truth', apparently, as perceived and evaluated by the narrating voice.

In some instances, though, the narrator appears to speak on behalf of the characters, voicing their assessments of happenings. This may be termed 'free indirect speech', a kind of fusion of narrator and character viewpoint. When the reader is told that Flora Donaldson 'didn't seem to know that she was white and you were black', the observation apparently stems from Ella, for she is evidently the 'you' of the clause.

On the other hand, it is sometimes unclear whether evaluative comment is coming from one of the story's characters through the narrator, or directly from the narrator. The linking of Daniel with the hero-worshipped singers might well be Ella's perception, drawn as she had been to his powerful presence in their courting days. But the hint of criticism in 'boy-men' could suggest *either* mixed feelings on Ella's part *or* the intervening voice of the story teller.

Still, as readers, wherever evaluations of a story's complication and its signs come from, we shall have to decide, consciously or unconsciously, whether or not we find their judgements trustworthy. If the narrator's or characters' assessments are not only consistent with the story overall but also match our own knowledge and experience, ideologies and myths, we are likely to accept them. We shall reject evaluation only if there is a mismatch, a disparity or contradiction.

A similar kind of comparative reasoning will be applied to aspects of the narrative which neither the narrating voice nor, directly or indirectly, the story's characters explain. In these cases we shall need to take over as narrators, completing the customary evaluative process ourselves.

We are likely to do this through a process of 'analogical reasoning', the strategy which, Robinson and Hawpe argue, is 'most often invoked during narrative thought' (1986: 118). In searching for causes and connections, identifying effects and explanations of narrated events, we (as tellers of our own tales or – as in the case of 'Something for the time being' – as 'co-narrators') 'probe memory for information that resembles the present case and satisfies tests of plausibility and coherence' (1986: 118).

In a sense, 'Something for the time being' provides its own analogues, for its own form offers comparisons from which to work (in addition to our own remembered life experience). That is, it begins with an episode between Ella and Daniel, goes on to a scene involving William and Madge, and then returns to Ella and Daniel. Each episode involves a couple. Each couple is engaged in a process of discovery: (as already mentioned, Madge comes to feel she has just begun to know her husband and Daniel eventually believes that Ella is revealing her true feelings for the first time). Furthermore, both wives are concerned – as discussed below – with the moment: they want to ensure 'something for the time being'. Both husbands, on the other hand, focus on the larger scheme of things in the longer term. (In these respects the short story recalls Gordimer's own comment on her novel *Burger's Daughter*, made in her booklet 'What happened to *Burger's Daughter*?' (quoted in Sampson 1992: 56): 'The theme of my novel is human conflict between the desire to live a personal, private life, and the rival claim of social responsibility to one's fellow-men – human advancement'.)

This symmetry draws attention to parallels in the behaviours of the two couples. As for contrasts, one couple is white, the other black; one couple is wealthy, the other poor; one couple is powerful, the other oppressed. Generally speaking, Gordimer does not, overtly at least, dictate reader evaluation of these pairings, of their similarities or their differences. The narrating voice draws no final conclusion. The narrative is not based on a beginning–middle–resolution model. What we make of match or mismatch depends on our own responses, weighing and balancing the signs we, influenced by comparisons remembered from our own life stories, perceive in these analogues.

Readers are involved in this kind of weighing and balancing with regard to the signs identified in relation to the Chadders' Chinese bowls and to Ella's sewing, together with the events and reactions linked to these objects.

EVERYTHING – OR SOMETHING?

From the points of view of the story's protagonists, signs associated with Ella's sewing, and with William's Chinese bowls, have indexical and metaphorical implications. As for the reader, comparisons and contrasts between the implications of the two clusters of signifiers are likely to be markers of a similarity in William and Daniel's philosophical and political viewpoints – but of a significant difference between the men's (similar) attitudes and those presently maintained by their two wives. These comparisons and contrasts seem to confirm and reinforce a message that both the men, though their relative achievements may differ, aim for 'everything'; both the women strive – though not with equal success – for 'something'.

Ella's piece of sewing is a dress for her daughter, who (because her mother must work and her father is liable to be away for long periods) lives in the country with her grandmother, a day's train journey from the city. Daniel first sees the material cut into pieces, the parts that will eventually make up the garment. Later, the pieces are together, the dress complete, and Ella nods with pleasure as Daniel compliments her on its appearance and the speed with which she has finished it. Yet her pleasure is apparently short-lived, spoilt when

> she noticed his forefinger run lightly along the line of braid round the neck . . . [for] the fact was that she had botched the neck . . . [and] the traces of failure that were always at the bottom of her cup tasted on her tongue again.

But why is Ella so sure the 'botched' neck is an index and reminder of a fundamental failure? That she does feel basically inadequate has already been suggested. The narrating voice, heard at the beginning of the story, interprets Ella's body language as an index of self-doubt, her fingers exploring the back of her neck 'as if feeling out some symptom in herself'.

> Her hand went on searching over her skin as if it must come soon, come anxiously, to the flaw, the sickness, the evidence of what was wrong with her.

Still, it is unclear whether it is the narrator, or Ella herself, who thinks of Daniel's reaction to the neckline in the following critical terms.

> Probably he was not even aware of it, or perhaps his instinct for what was true – the plumb line, the coin with the right ring – led him absently to it.

The metaphor sounds too literary for Ella's private thoughts, more like the narrator's perception of them. Nevertheless, whoever is speaking, these words are likely to recall for the reader Ella's memories of her early days with Daniel, memories of a grand vision which, compared with the present reality, no doubt explain her confusion and harsh self-judgement.

She had known when she married him that he was a political man; she had been proud of him because he didn't merely want something for himself, like other young men she knew, but everything, and for *the people*. . . . She knew that everything wasn't like something – a hand-out, a wangled privilege, a trinket you could hold. She would never get something from him.

She had known all of this – once. But now, 'on this Saturday afternoon, all these things that she knew had deserted her'. So Ella blames herself for her growing inability, in the face of lost jobs and a daughter living miles away, to understand her husband's perspective. For Daniel is still motivated by a grand vision, grand in extent and completeness. Ella would not, therefore, expect him to tolerate the 'imperfect' – including, particularly as a symptom and index of much deeper imperfection, a flawed neckline. His fingers running along the edge of the dress must have seemed to her a recognition of her basic inadequacy and, thus, a sign of his criticism. This small episode is a kind of *metonym* (the part standing for the whole) of their flawed relationship.

At least, this is how Ella apparently sees it. But it is not absolutely certain that, consciously at any rate, Daniel invests the incident with similar meaning: 'Probably he was not even aware of it, or perhaps his instinct for what was true . . . led him absently to [the botched neck]'.

In the case of the Chinese bowls, however, the reader is told quite clearly that husband and wife do not find in them the same significance. Their contrasting responses are revealing compared to Ella and perhaps Daniel's reactions to the sewing.

For example, a resemblance between Daniel and William Chadders is signalled in William's feeling about the set of bowls. He had bought them in London but the set is now – for William if for no one else – 'flawed', because one of the bowls is broken. In William's view, the set's original 'unity had', *metaphorically*, 'illustrated certain philosophical concepts'. These concepts presumably relate to completeness, the achievement of wholeness and balance. For, like Daniel striving for 'everything', William worked to a grand scheme. He had 'views', views on 'the immorality and absurdity of the colour bar', and these were supported by his knowledge of great thinkers on politics, history, economics and so on. He started from these 'first principles', translating them from theory into practice through initiating and partly financing a scheme to set up an all-African trust company and investment corporation.

Daniel might have envied William his ability to do so from 'a boardroom, fifteen floors above life in the streets'. For whilst Daniel's own colleagues, listening to his words in a meeting, accepted '*in principle*' that in future they would not take bail, he is scathingly uncertain that they will carry out their intentions: 'That was language [Tsolo] understood. . . . Yes, it's easy to accept in principle. We'll see.' '*We'll see*' because the translation of language into action is a different matter from intellectual agreement. In prison it seems possible to think and plan clearly. Outside it is different.

> You come out and you think there's everybody waiting for you. The truth is, there isn't anybody. You think straight in prison because you've got nothing to lose. Nobody thinks straight, outside.

And here, for all their similarity, is a difference between William and Daniel. It would appear (bearing in mind as reader knowledge of apartheid from outside the story together with that signalled in its own analogues) that, although these two men may try to live by similar philosophies, William, in company with his white and affluent colleagues, has power to act. Daniel and his supporters, given the very different circumstances of their black existence, do not. Ella might have endorsed this distinction, being fully aware of her own reality's limitations.

> All that she could understand was the one room, the child growing up far away in the mud house, and the fact that you couldn't keep a job if you kept being away from work for weeks at a time.

But Ella would no doubt have related any such endorsement to her sense of personal failure, failure which prevents her from supporting her husband as once she had. In her own view – *because* all she now understands are practicalities and limitations – she cannot think 'straight' (as Daniel felt he could in prison): she believes she has 'lost her wits'.

Madge Chadders would surely not have agreed. Madge is not particularly concerned with thinking 'straight', if that means theories, principles and grand designs, and her treatment of the broken Chinese bowl is symbolic of the pragmatism she prefers. It is an indication of her attitude that something, anything, is better than nothing, for she has patiently glued its pieces together and is perfectly satisfied with her efforts: the set, as a set, has no metaphorical significance for her.

Its parts, on the other hand – if she had thought consciously in metaphorical terms – would have been significant. For Madge would not hesitate, if she believed it necessary, to try to change a person's attitude, a part of their make-up. In the same way that she saw each single Chinese bowl as having status and value aside from the set, she would see the attitude as an independent thing, set apart from the remainder of the personality. But William's view would be quite different, for he would see an attitude rather as he saw each bowl, 'as a cell in the organism of personality, whose whole structure would have to regroup itself round the change'. Consequently he loved Madge's idiosyncrasies: 'he was not fool enough to want to change in any way the person who had enchanted him just as she was'. And his belief in the integrity of personality no doubt explains his discomfort in offering Daniel a cleaner's job which does not match his skills and experience.

Madge, however, feels that, though Daniel was a skilled packer of china, even an unskilled job should be offered to him since to her 'anything is better than nothing'. Similarly, in response to her abhorrence of the colour bar, she would do anything rather than nothing, something rather than everything. She would march, provide accommodation, carry banners, and (unlike her husband) never consider the varying degrees of usefulness in these acts.

So Madge would certainly not have believed Ella to be witless. She would not regard pragmatism as failure, or reject spontaneous and feeling responses as in some way inadequate. But then Madge, unlike Ella, seems to have a powerful self-confidence, a confidence no doubt confirmed, to date, by William's approval of her idiosyncrasies. Above all, in addition to this strength derived from her personal life, Madge has the power that comes with relative social and political security. She could generally behave much as she wanted, act immediately, do 'something' – anything – in order 'to express what she felt'. Ella's outward behaviour cannot so readily, in her very different circumstances, be an index of her psychology as well as a sign of opposition to apartheid and its consequences. One thing she understands – feels deeply, whatever may confuse her intellectually – is her child's absence. But, given her race, her husband's political position, her family's poverty and her own self-doubt – all of these interrelated – Ella is powerless to act in order to express her feeling (except in the unassertive exploring of her hairline) let alone to alleviate the immediate situation.

So here again, as in William and Daniel's case, race makes a difference between otherwise similar personalities. The Chadders' reactions to the meanings of the broken china, together with Ella's feeling about Daniel's assumed response to the implications of the child's dress, emphasize similarities between the two men, and between the two women. They also underline a fundamental distinction between the husbands and the wives: the men and the women do not interpret signs of meaning in the same way. These contrasts and comparisons seem to relate to gender and role and appear to exist largely independent of race. However, the effects of these people's attitudes and behaviour *do* (the story's own analogues, and those I as reader bring to bear from outside the narrative, suggest) depend in large measure upon their race and their consequent access to power. Madge can achieve and be content with something. Her husband can afford, politically, psychologically and financially, to aim for everything. Daniel can aim for everything but cannot achieve. Ella cannot even secure something for the time being.

There are further comparisons and contrasts to be noted between the men and the women in the story, particularly in the ways in which the two couples communicate with each other in conversation, and in the degrees of understanding – and misunderstanding – they reach through the signifiers of their discourse.

DIFFERENCE OF OPINION

There seems to be a difference between the two couples' interactive language use. This may, I shall suggest, be a superficial distinction: behind the contrasts there could, once more, be similarities. Nevertheless, while Ella and Daniel exchange little conversation, at least in the brief glimpses we are given, Madge and William talk constantly to each other.

For instance, at the beginning of the story, Daniel's interpretation of his talk with his wife as a 'discussion' does not match the narrator's assessment of the situation, and probably not his wife's. For Ella says little, offering Daniel more tea 'without speaking'. She does not even provide him with minimal supporting responses, the sort of brief utterances we can make to encourage a speaker to continue: *I see, Go on, Is that right?* As a result Ella's

> listening was very demanding; when he stopped at the end of a supposition or a suggestion, her silence made the stop inconclusive. He had to take up again what he had said, carry it – where?

In consequence, Daniel is forced to resort to a 'tag question', a query 'tagged on' to the end of a statement. He remarks that although he has finally lost the job which had been kept for him through three or four previous spells in prison, he will find another: 'Well, what the hell, I'll get something else' he insists. However, when Ella makes no comment he adds (tags on) 'Hey?', as if requesting confirmation.

Feminist thinking on language had suggested that women use such tags much more than men. The explanation offered was that the language manoeuvre is a sign of female insecurity, a need for confirmation, a lack of belief in the statement just made. In fact, however, research has shown men using them in this way as much and sometimes more than women – and women, more than men, use them as a confident facilitating strategy (Holmes 1984). In the episode just described, however, Daniel's question does not inspire a spoken answer. Ella remains silent and merely shrugs her shoulders.

By contrast to Ella and Daniel, the Chadders talk a great deal, to each other and to other people too. Well, language – the powers of logic, discussion, clarification, administration, protest – is perceived by them to be important, particularly by William who, as already noted, reads widely, developing his own theories from the words of 'great thinkers'. Besides, his words in the boardroom produce change whilst, as already noted, Daniel is less sure that words, accepted 'in principle', will lead to action. Madge too acknowledges the power of the word, carrying messages of protest on sandwich boards (a protest moreover about the passing of a bill, by definition authoritative, controlling language), or providing a young African with the means to write. And now, when they first appear in the story, William has just finished a telephone call, made by Flora Donaldson to ask him for a job for Daniel. William tells Madge that he wishes she would explain to Flora his belief that he has no suitable position to offer. Madge wants explanations too, for Daniel from William, to show that William does not regard the cleaner's job as adequate. And, though reluctantly, William does respond.

Madge's conversational tactics to secure such replies are similar to those practised by Daniel, and later by Ella, in the face of their partner's uncommunicativeness. For these tactics are based upon questions, some of them of Daniel's tag variety. But, though William, unlike Ella, may answer his partner's queries, the degree to which understanding is increased through these particular language exchanges – and for whom – is debatable. Further, though a language tactic can be controlling to the extent that it draws response, real power may yet remain with the respondent.

To begin with, as the Chadders drive out for the evening, William is preoccupied, thinking about the significance of his Chinese bowls, so Madge has to ask three questions before she gets any spoken reply at all: 'Will you see that chap?. . . What was his name?. . . See him yourself?' When William finally speaks he answers, but only obliquely.

Now, Grice (1975) has identified certain 'maxims' to which we adhere in smooth-running conversations (also see chapter 8). One of them is the maxim of *relevance*, another that of *quantity* for, in co-operative conversations, we usually respond to our co-conversationalist with replies that are relevant to a recently preceding utterance and which provide an adequate amount of information. But of course our conversations are frequently far from co-operative and William's first remark, referring to the man in question but not precisely to Madge's concern about seeing him personally, is only just relevant: 'I'll have to leave it to the works manager to find something for him to do.'

Madge, playing the conversation game more helpfully (in the Gricean sense) than William, responds to this statement with perfect relevance: 'I know.' Still, she is not to be deflected from her original line of enquiry and she goes on to phrase an imperative with the 'force' of a query: 'But see him yourself, too?'. This query, which Gordimer indicates in writing with a question mark, is presumably implied, as she speaks, in Madge's sound of voice. Intonation, stress and paralinguistic features – as discussed in chapter 3 – are signs of meaning as well as words and syntax and, indeed, can override these with what Searle (1969) called their 'force'.

Yet Madge's implied question is still not rewarded with a straight answer. Instead, William asks a question himself – 'Why?' – taking the initiative from Madge by placing her in the position of having to give answers. Moreover, his manner in so doing seems to her 'indulgent', embarrassing her and forcing her to 'wheedle'. In consequence, when William finally agrees to Madge's request it appears he does so merely to humour her.

All in all, then, Madge's queries are powerful to the extent they provoke language and even a promise of the action she wants. But, forcing her into childish wheedling rather than entering into a discussion on equal terms, William's rather patronizing attitude weakens his wife in some way. Besides, his responses suggest that he does not really understand, certainly does not support, what lies behind Madge's questions.

A similar set of manoeuvres takes place the following day. William tells Madge that he has had to speak to Daniel about his Congress button. 'What about his Congress button?', she asks. But William does not give a straight answer, at least not one with sufficient quantity: 'He was wearing one.' So Madge has to ask again: 'I know, but what did you have to speak to him about it for?' William repeats that Daniel was wearing the button, adding that he did so in the workshop and all day. But even this additional information is short on the quantity Madge wants and she has to ask yet another question: 'Well, what about it?' In response William offers just a bit more of a reason: 'You can't wear a button like that among the men in the workshop.' Madge is still not satisfied – perhaps because she has known, and abhorred, the complete answer all along but is determined that William will bring it into the open: 'And why can't you?', she asks.

Yet even now Madge is not answered fully so that the manner of William's responses (Grice describes two other maxims, one of *manner* – we generally try not to be ambiguous, but to be clear and to the point – and one of *quality* – in principle we do not make statements we know to be false) begins to seem not simply dilatory and inattentive but deliberately unco-operative. For a start, her husband makes a statement with which Madge disagrees – and then wrong-foots her by accepting the words, but surely not the implications, of her query–contradiction:

(Madge) 'But he's not there *representing* anything, he's there as a workman?'

(William) 'Exactly'.

Thereafter there is no attempt either to avoid the issue or to appear to be taking part in a discussion: William flatly denies Madge's assertions, now and when she picks up the conversation again a little later. Their exchange culminates in a monologue from William, finally producing the information Madge has been seeking for several minutes. She does not accept his arguments, but William brushes aside her dissent: '"If you make up your mind not to understand, you don't, and there it is", he said indulgently.'

Indulgently: William's manner is once again patronizing, just as on the previous day. It seems that it is he who is determined not to understand, not to consider an alternative perception. On the other hand, in a sense Madge *has* made up her mind not to comprehend – at least, not to comprehend understandings alternative to her own. She is not setting William's difficulty in the broader picture (just as she did not see the Chinese bowl as one part of a set). She is refusing to see its significance in relation to the work he has created for the black community. Madge does not acknowledge that – whilst he might prefer everything to her anything – her husband would certainly agree with her that 'nothing' is unacceptable. So there appears, for all its words, to be little more in the way of mutually supportive, productively illuminating 'discussion' in the Chadders' conversation than there was in Daniel and Ella's much sparser exchange at the start of the story.

Nevertheless, Madge believes she is 'beginning to get to know' her husband at last. And enlightenment, of sorts, also comes to Daniel and Ella in the final conversation of the story. Daniel begins it, telling a small anecdote, but Ella remains silent, not 'badgering' him (for she 'had an almost Oriental delicacy') until he is seated and ready to eat.

Then, in order to secure attention and response, she must, like Madge, ask a series of questions – 'How did the job go?. . . Didn't you get it?. . . They don't want you to come back tomorrow?' – before Daniel begins to answer her directly and fully. In the meantime she has to watch his face for additional indexes of meaning until, finally, Daniel does explain about the badge.

When he does so, Ella is at first speechless. In her anxiety she begins once more to finger the back of her neck, just as she did at the beginning of the narrative. The movement, and a suggestion of tears, goad Daniel to tell her to stop exploring her skin 'like a monkey catching lice'. And now, denied this unassertive release of feeling, Ella, at last, expresses herself in plain words: '"You couldn't put it in your pocket, for the day", she said wildly, grimacing at the bitterness of malice towards him.'

Daniel is incensed. He believes that Ella has finally said what he has been expecting her to say 'for five years'. He cannot mean he has feared her precise words of course, for the badge incident has only just occurred. But his wife's outburst seems to him to mean that he can no longer take her approval and her support for granted.

Yet has Daniel understood Ella properly, any more than Madge had really learned something about William? Is Daniel perhaps confusing Ella's bewildered misery of 'the time being', her despair at the present lack of money and security, with an underlying sympathy for him 'in principle'? Has he perhaps forgotten what he had realized at his meeting with Tsolo, that principles and pragmatism may be at odds? In any event, although the idea of Ella's crying had at first exasperated him, the tears now seem to Daniel an index of an Ella he can understand – understand and thus, ignoring any complexities in her thinking and feeling, cope with. Because, now, Daniel can speak to his wife in 'a kindly voice' and, 'kneading her shoulder with spread fingers', touching her with a kind of firm confidence, he can remark, 'You're just like any other woman.' It would seem the tears have offered Daniel a way back to a semblance of normality and, particularly, to a position of power – a position which, presumably, had allowed him to believe that the one-sided discourse with which he begins the story is 'discussion' with Ella.

So here again, as in the case of William and Madge, there seems to be an inability to accept a difference of needs and attitudes (differences, to do with achieving 'everything' or 'something for the time being', which the metaphor of the Chinese bowls and the incident with the sewing appear to demonstrate). In both cases the women and the men believe their partners are at fault. In neither case does husband *or* wife really hear what the other is saying. Ella does not try to talk and find out.

Madge talks but she does not exchange views. The two men do not listen but patronize.

In Daniel's case his indulgent stereotyping is perhaps the worst of insults, coming from the man Ella had always believed special because he wanted the best, had wanted not just anything, but everything. For in choosing her she might once have felt complimented, singled out and respected – the signs of her individuality recognized, understood and valued.

Still, this last paragraph is evaluative speculation that I, the reader, bring to bear on the narrative. We are not told precisely how Ella herself feels in the final moments of the narrative but are left to draw our own conclusions from the signs we perceive in the story, those provided by the couples and through the narrator's telling of their tale, the narrative's judgements, and selection and arrangement of analogues. Yet whether an individual reader comprehends their meaning any better than its two couples cannot be certain.

Without doubt, we can, in the real world outside fiction, invite and even force signs of meaning from each other, just as Madge and Ella eventually provoke responses from their husbands. But how often do they, or we, clearly recognize signals, let alone arrive at the meaning understood by their initiators? True, when William stands naked before Madge, the events of his life are revealed to her in the scars on his body, for she knows the history of each of these indexes. But the indexical and symbolic signifiers of meaning we regularly communicate are rarely as uncomplicated in their reference and implication as these simple indicators. Besides, our interpretations are themselves subject to the shaping pressures of logonomic systems and of personal viewpoint. I am perhaps influenced by my own gender in responding to the male and the female behaviour in the story, for I feel most sympathy for Ella, believing her to be the most misunderstood of the four protagonists, the most powerless to make herself understood. As for the fictional Madge and William, they do not see the same significances in the badge or in the Chinese bowls. Daniel may or may not 'read' the 'botched' neckline as Ella does. The conversations of both couples are neither ideally co-operative nor mutually revealing. For the cultural and social forces of gender and of race, as well as individual personality, apparently play their part in shaping – and obfuscating – the meanings of these four people.

The complexities of communication in Gordimer's fictional story thus exemplify the subtle and powerful resources (discussed throughout *Literature about Language*) on which we draw, in the real world, to signal meaning. They also appear to reflect the difficulties of comprehension which, in reality, and despite the power that is language, confuse and constrain us.

Nadine Gordimer sent a letter to her friend Anthony Sampson (quoted in Sampson 1992: 54). It is about communication in this real world, for in it she describes Nelson Mandela's Rivonia trial, telling of her response to the closing words of his famous speech when he spoke of 'an ideal for which I am prepared to die'. Gordimer wrote:

> only at the end did the man come through; and when he had spoken that last sentence the strangest and most quietly moving sound I have heard from human throats came from the 'black' side of the court audience. It was short, sharp and terrible; something between a sigh and a groan. Afterwards, silence.

Though Mandela had been obliged by processes of law to speak, to try to convey meaning, to communicate himself and his position, only at the end, in Gordimer's view, did he really 'come through'. But, even then, did everyone in the courtroom understand him as Gordimer did? How many heard in the same way as she did, and so were moved as she was by meaning in the signs of the 'black' sound and the black silence?

SUGGESTIONS FOR FURTHER WORK

1 Read Brian Moore's novel *The Catholics* (1972). Do you think that, like Nadine Gordimer's story, this novel includes communication amongst its themes? I suggest that it draws attention to a variety of signifiers. These include the arbitrary symbols of language, and its imagery, in Latin and in English. There are also the signifiers of clothing, of body language and of natural phenomena. These signifiers, particularly those of language, are used in different forms and functions of communication. For example, there are prayers, rituals, confessions; records; guides, suggestions, explanations; instructions, orders, edicts; responses. These are transmitted in a variety of ways, for example, privately or publicly, face to face, on paper, over the telephone, by loud speaker, or by television. And, I suggest, reactions and understandings are various. They depend sometimes upon faith, sometimes upon intuition, sometimes upon interpretation. There is resistance and there is acceptance. Do you yourself recognize in the novel this variety of ways of meaning, communication and comprehension? If so, how do they relate to your own understanding of *The Catholics*?

2 Select, in small groups, a magazine cover, or an advertisement, or a picture, a badge, a scene from television – anything that interests you.

Then, first, without consulting others in your group, write a paragraph or two explaining what the chosen 'text' means to you personally. Bear in mind its visual images, body language and language itself. What do its icons and indexes, symbolic language and metaphors tell you? Now, second and again on your own, try to work out, and then write a paragraph about, what ideologies and myths you believe, on reflection (for they are not necessarily at the forefront of your consciousness), lie behind your personal understanding of your chosen text. Finally, exchange your ideas with someone else in your group, or discuss them with the group as a whole.

Have you understood the picture, scene or whatever in much the same way? If not, why might this be? Are you perhaps coming from very different ideological positions? If you have *not* understood the text in the same way, could serious problems of communication arise as a result? Would there be any ways of preventing such misunderstanding?

If all of you *do* comprehend your chosen text similarly, can you envisage others outside your group finding different meanings to its signifiers? If so, who? Why?

Notes

1 THE HUMAN CAPACITY FOR LANGUAGE

1 Although the origins of human language are in reality unclear, *The Inheritors* implies the kind of beginnings imagined by the eighteenth-century linguistic theorist, the abbé de Condillac, whose ideas are discussed by T.J. Taylor (1989: 289–97). Condillac suggested that, at the dawn of language, people responded to what he called *accidental* signs (like the appearance of a wolf, or a darkness in the sky) with automatic sensations like discomfort, fear, relief. People came to compare and contrast the degree and quality of their feeling responses and they took appropriate action: say, fleeing from a dangerous wolf, searching for food when gnawing in the stomach became intense – and sometimes making cries, moans, and groans (like Nil's). But none of these reactions was planned. All, like their triggers, were 'accidental'. However, Condillac believed that if people saw again a place, or thing, which had previously frightened or interested them, then they would repeat the noises they had made on that earlier occasion. They would, that is, mimic the sounds voluntarily. (Lok demonstrates this kind of voluntary mimicking. Seeing ravens floating below the trail on the cliff he, says Golding (25), 'remembered how the ravens sounded. He flapped at them with his arms. "Kwak!"' he said – just as he must have muttered once before.) Eventually, Condillac argued, these mimicked sound responses became habitual, recalled voluntarily and readily. The accumulation of vocabulary had thus begun – and, with it, real control of the environment: Condillac wrote (Taylor 1989: 290), 'How can the mind of man gain control of its own materials, that is, of its sensations and operations? Gestures, sounds, numbers, and letters: only with instruments as foreign to our ideas as these can we put our ideas to work.' Condillac's next stage in his imagined development of language – a stage essential for greater control of the environment and thus for evolution – is the decomposition of the 'tableaux' represented by gestures and cries. (It will be remembered that the people struggle to make sense of pictures and their component parts.) Condillac wrote (Taylor 1989: 296):

> man will sooner or later notice that he never understands others better than when he has decomposed their gestures. Consequently, he can notice that, to make himself understood, he needs to decompose his own

gestures. .... For him, the language of gesture naturally becomes an analytic method. I say *method* because the succession of movements will not be made arbitrarily and without rules.

His reference to rules seems to imply syntactic structuring. Further, Condillac may also have hinted at narrative organization in his description of speaking, for he wrote: 'Although a thought may not be linear in the mind, it is so in discourse, where it is decomposed into as many components as it contains ideas.... Thinking then becomes an art, and this art is the art of speaking' (Taylor 1989: 292).

4 MAKING MEANING

1 Paul Doust, who works in HIV care, points out that the term ARC is no longer in general use and that he does not hear stages referred to very often. I believe the alternative is to speak of decreased resistance to illnesses, one of which may be fatal, following HIV infection.

2 Paul Doust suggests that the tendency to personify the virus – either by implication when speaking of 'invasion by the virus', or in the visual images sometimes used in AIDS information material – suggests a thinking, reasoning, entity. And, if a virus can reason it can choose this person and not another to infect, decide that this person and not another may be, perhaps deserves to be, infected. There are clearly links here with possible entailments of the plague metaphor, suggesting that only certain kinds of people will become ill.

5 THE NARRATIVE ART OF LANGUAGE

1 Sutton-Smith refers to cross-cultural evidence that in some societies there exists no such confidence in the ability to overcome the fates. In these cultures, stories seem to remain at the first or second western level.

6 STANDARD AND NON-STANDARD ENGLISH

1 The eclogues include 'The common a-took in' (Jones 1962: 158), 'Two farms in woone' (160), 'Rusticus res politicas animadvertens' (487) and 'The times' (226) which is critical of the Chartists. Some of Barnes' prose work deals with similar themes, for example his 'Humilis domus' articles, which appeared in 1849, in April and May editions of the *Poole and Dorset Herald*, and his *Views of Labour and Gold* (1859) which contains some of these articles. Christopher Wrigley discusses the poems and the prose in his introduction to *William Barnes, the Dorset Poet* (1984).

2 *A Philological Grammar* (1854) and *A Grammar and Glossary of the Dorset Dialect* (1863) are relevant to the Blackmore dialect but Barnes also wrote many articles detailing his underlying linguistic philosophy. These include several published in the *Gentleman's Magazine*, for example 'On the origin of language' (August 1832: 128–30), 'Education in words and things' (January 1841: 22) and others in *MacMillan's Magazine*, including 'The old bardic poetry' (August 1867: 306–17).

3 Barnes believed this was partly because English, the Standard variety in particular, had been infiltrated by too much Latin and French and needed to reassert its Anglo-Saxon roots. For, whereas Swift had seemed to approve the best of Latin and French influence, Barnes remarked in the *Gentleman's Magazine* (June 1830: 501–3). 'I cannot believe that the word "portfeuille" expresses (to an Englishman) the use of the thing better than the word "papercase"'. In consequence, though he spoke and taught his pupils in a kind of Standard English, he removed from it as far as possible words of Latin or French derivation, substituting compounds he derived from words of Anglo-Saxon origin (for example, *riding-bag* for *portmanteau* and *build-cutter* for *sculptor*). He believed the Dorset dialect was a more direct descendant of Saxon and in this respect 'purer' than the Standard. In fact, of course, even Barnes' Blackmore speakers would have been familiar with the word *beef*, yet it is of Norman origin and not Anglo-Saxon, *sugar* is a descendant of Sanskrit, *tea* of Chinese.

7 THE LANGUAGE OF WOMEN AND MEN

1 Some of Lacan's arguments are in translation in Sheridan 1977 and an extremely helpful explanation of their relationship to feminism can be found in Cameron 1985.
2 Other work by Anna Wickham appeared in *The Little Old House* (Poetry Bookshop: 1921). In 1971 Chatto and Windus brought out *Selected Poems* and in 1984 Virago published poetry, prose and an autobiographical fragment.

8 THE POWER OF DISCOURSE

1 Magistrates have explained to me that a broader mix is aimed for but in general it is representatives of the middle class who are able to take time from work and make themselves available for service.

References

Abbot, C. (ed.) (1955) *The Letters of Gerard Manley Hopkins to Robert Bridges*, London: Oxford University Press.

Aitchison, J. (1987) *Teach Yourself Linguistics* (3rd edn), Sevenoaks: Hodder & Stoughton.

—— (1989) *The Articulate Mammal* (3rd edn), London: Unwin Hyman.

Bain, R. (1991) *Reflections: Talking about Language*, Sevenoaks: Hodder & Stoughton.

Bally, C., Sechehaye, A. and Reidlinger, A. (eds) (1964/1966) *Course in General Linguistics: Ferdinand de Saussure*, London, Fontana, 1964; New York: McGraw-Hill, 1966.

Barnes, W. (1830) 'Corruptions of the English language', *Gentleman's Magazine*, June, 501–3.

—— (1841) 'English philology', *Gentleman's Magazine*, May: 510–11.

—— (1844) *Poems of Rural Life in the Dorset Dialect*, with Dissertation and Glossary, London: John Russell Smith.

—— (1847) *Poems of Rural Life in the Dorset Dialect*, second edition with Dissertation and Glossary enlarged (third and fourth editions were printed in 1862 and 1866 without Dissertation and Glossary), London: John Russell Smith.

—— (1854) *A Philological Grammar*, London: John Russell Smith.

—— (1859) *Views of Labour and Gold*, London: John Russell Smith.

—— (1863) *A Grammar and Glossary of the Dorset Dialect*, Berlin: A. Asher.

Barrell, J. and Bull, J. (eds) (1982) *The Penguin Book of English Pastoral Verse*, Harmondsworth: Penguin.

Barthes, R. (1973) *Mythologies*, London: Paladin.

Biber, D. and Finegan, E. (1989) 'Styles of stance in English: lexical and grammatical marking of evidentiality and affect', *Text* 9 (1): 93–124.

Bruner, J. (1986) *Actual Minds, Possible Worlds*, Cambridge, Mass.: Harvard University Press.

Cameron, D. (1985) *Feminism and Linguistic Theory*, London: Macmillan.

—— (ed.) (1990), *The Feminist Critique of Language*. London: Routledge.

Campion, G.E. (1969) *A Tennyson Dialect Glossary with the Dialect Poems*, Lincoln: The Lincolnshire Association.

Carroll, J.B. and Wiley, J. (eds) (1956), *Language, Thought and Reality: Selected Writings of Benjamin Lee Whorf*, Cambridge, Mass., and New York: MIT Press.

Carter, R. (1982a) *Language and Literature: an Introductory Reader in Stylistics*, London: Allen & Unwin.

—— (ed.) (1982b) *Linguistics and the Teacher*, London: Routledge & Kegan Paul.

Cassirer, E. (1946) *Language and Myth*, trans. S. Langer, New York: Dover.

Chomsky, N. (1957) *Syntactic Structures*, The Hague: Mouton.

—— (1959) Review of Skinner's *Verbal Behaviour*, *Language*, 35: 26–58

—— (1965) *Aspects of the Theory of Syntax*, Cambridge, Mass.: MIT Press.

—— (1980) *Rules and Representations*, Oxford: Basil Blackwell.

Coates, J. (1986) *Women, Men and Language*, Harlow: Longman.

Coates, J. and Cameron, D. (eds) (1988) *Women in their Speech Communities*, Harlow: Longman.

Crowley, T. (1991) *Proper English?*, London: Routledge.

Crystal, D. (1988) *Rediscover Grammar with David Crystal*, London: Longman.

Elyot, T. (1970, first published 1531) *The Governour*, Menston, Yorks: The Scolar Press.

Emler, N. (1990) 'A social psychology of reputation', in W. Stroebe and M. Henstone (eds) *European Review of Social Psychology*, vol. 1, Chichester: Wiley.

Fairclough, N. (1989) *Language and Power*, Harlow: Longman.

Firmage, G.J. (ed.) (1981) *E.E. Cummings, Complete Poems: 1910–1962*, vol. 1, London: Granada.

Fishman, P. (1980) 'Conversational insecurity', in H. Giles, W.P. Robinson and P.M. Smith (eds) *Language: Social Psychological Perspectives*, Oxford: Pergamon Press.

Fiske, J. (1982) *Introduction to Communication Studies*, London and New York: Routledge.

Fowler, R. (1981) *Literature as Social Discourse*, London: Batsford.

Friedan, B. (1963) *The Feminine Mystique*, London: Gollancz.

Gibson, J. (ed.) (1976) *The Complete Poems of Thomas Hardy*, London: Macmillan.

Golding, W. (1961, first published 1955) *The Inheritors*, London and Boston: Faber & Faber.

Gordimer, N. (1983) *Selected Stories*, Harmondsworth: Penguin.

Greimas, A. (1966) *Sémantique structurale*, Paris: Larousse.

Grice, H.P. (1975) 'Logic and conversation', in P. Cole and J.L. Morgan (eds) *Syntax and Semantics*, vol. 3, London: Academic Press.

Habermas J. (1984) *The Theory of Communicative Action*, vol. 1, London: Heinemann.

Halliday, M.A.K. (1973) *Exploration in the Functions of Language*, London: Edward Arnold.

—— (1978) *Language as Social Semiotic*, London: Edward Arnold.

Hamilton, R. (1985) *The Last Jockey*, Frome, Somerset: Bran's Head Books.

Hardy, F.E. (1962) *The Life of Thomas Hardy, 1840–1928*, Macmillan, London.

Hardy, T. (1908) *Select Poems of William Barnes*, Oxford: Henry Frowde.

—— (1974, first published 1891), *Tess of the d'Urbervilles*, London: Macmillan.

—— (1978, first published 1886), *The Mayor of Casterbridge*, Harmondsworth: Penguin.

Harris, S. (1984) 'Questions as a mode of control in magistrates courts', *International Journal of the Sociology of Language*, 49: 5–27.

—— (1988) 'Court discourse as genre' in R.P. Fawcett and D.J. Young (eds) *New Developments in Systemic Linguistics* vol. 2: *Theory and Application*, 94–115, London, Pinter.

—— (1989) 'Defendant resistance to power and control in court', in H. Coleman (ed.) *Working with Language*, Berlin: Mouton de Gruyter.

—— (forthcoming) 'Ideological exchanges in British magistrates courts', unpublished paper, Nottingham Trent University, to appear in John Gibbons (ed.) *Language and the Law*, London: Longman.

—— (ms.) 'Pragmatics and power', unpublished paper Nottingham Trent University.

Haynes, J. (1989) *Introducing Stylistics*, London: Unwin Hyman.

Hayward, J. (ed.) (1949) *Selected Prose Works of Jonathan Swift*, London: The Cresset Press.

Helms, J. (ed.) (1967) *Essays on the Verbal and Visual Arts*, Seattle: University of Washington Press.

Hertz, A. (1985) 'The hallowed pleäces of William Barnes', *Victorian Poetry*, 23 (2): 109–214.

Hockett, C. and Altmann, S. (1968) 'A note on design features', in T. Sebeok (ed.) *Animal Communication: Techniques of Study and Results of Research*, Bloomington: Indiana Press.

Hodge, R. and Kress, G. (1988) *Social Semiotics*, Cambridge: Polity Press in association with Basil Blackwell.

Holmes, J. (1984) 'Hedging your bets and sitting on the fence: some evidence for hedges as support structures', *Te Reo*, 27: 47–62.

Honey, J. (1989) *Does Accent Matter? The Pygmalion Factor*, London: Faber & Faber.

Jennings, E. (1989) *Tributes*, Manchester: Carcanet Press.

Jespersen, O. (1922) *Language, its Nature, Development and Origin*, London: George Allen & Unwin.

Johnson, T.H. (ed.) (1976) *The Complete Poems of Emily Dickinson*, Boston: Little, Brown and Company.

Johnson, T.H. (ed.) (1983) *The Poems of Emily Dickinson*, vol.2, Cambridge, Mass.: The Belknap Press of Harvard University Press.

Jones, B. (1962) *The Poems of William Barnes*, 2 vols, Sussex: Centaur Press.

Joyce, J. (1977, first published 1914) *Dubliners*, St Albans: Triad/Panther Books.

Kaplan, C. (1986) *Sea Changes*, London: Verso.

Key, M.R. (1975) *Male/Female Language*, Metuchen, Scarecrow Press.

Kingman, Sir J. (1988) *Report of the Committee of Inquiry into the Teaching of English*: London: Her Majesty's Stationery Office.

Kress, G. (1985) 'Ideological structures in discourse', in T. van Dijk (ed.) *Discourse and Communication*, Berlin: Walter de Gruyter.

Kress, G. and Hodge, R. (1979) *Language as Ideology*, London: Routledge & Kegan Paul.

Labov, W. (1969) 'The logic of nonstandard English', *Georgetown Monographs on Language and Linguistics*, vol. 22: 1–31.

—— (1972) *Language in the Inner City*, Philadelphia: University of Washington Press.

Labov, W. and Fanshel, D. (1977) *Therapeutic Discourse*, Orlando: Academic Press.

Labov, W. and Waletsky J. (1967) 'Narrative analysis: oral versions of personal experience', in J. Helms (ed.) *Essays on the Verbal and Visual Arts*, Seattle: University of Washington Press.

Lakoff, G. and Johnson, M. (1980) *Metaphors we Live by*, Chicago and London: The University of Chicago Press.

Landar, H., Ervin, S.M. and Horowitz, A.E. (1960) 'Navaho Colour Categories', *Language*, 36: 368–82.

Leonard, T. (1984) *Intimate Voices: 1965–1983*, Newcastle-upon-Tyne: Galloping Dog Press.

—— (1986) *Situations Theoretical and Contemporary*, Newcastle-upon-Tyne: Galloping Dog Press.

Levy, W.T. (1960) *William Barnes, the Man and the Poet*, Dorchester: Longmans.

Lieberman, P. (1984) *The Biology and Evolution of Language*, Harvard: Harvard University Press.

Lodge, D. (1989) *Nice Work*, Harmondsworth: Penguin.

Lyons, J. (1977) *Semantics*, 2 vols, Cambridge: Cambridge University Press.

MacKenzie, N. (ed.) (1990) *The Poetical Works of Gerard Manley Hopkins*, Oxford: Clarendon Press.

Mancuso, J.C. (1986) 'The acquisition and use of narrative grammar structure', in T.R. Sarbin (ed.) *Narrative Psychology: the Storied Nature of Human Conduct*, New York: Praeger.

Mandelbaum, G. (ed.) (1949) *Selected writings of Edward Sapir in Language, Culture and Personality*, Berkeley and Los Angeles: University of California Press.

Mandler, J.M. (1984) *Scripts, Stories and Scenes: Aspects of Schema Theory*, Hillsdale, N.J.: Lawrence Erlbaum Associates.

Maranda, E.K. and Maranda P. (1970) *Structural Models in Folklore and Transformational Essays*, The Hague: Mouton.

Marmaridou, A.S.S. (1989) 'Proper names in communication', *Journal of Linguistics*, September, 355–72.

Massingham, H.J. (1942) 'William Barnes', *Time and Tide*, 16 May: 408–10.

Mehler, J., Jusczyk, P., Lambertz, G. and Halsted N. (1988) 'A precusor of language acquisition in young infants', *Cognition*, 29: 143–78.

Moi T. (1986) *The Kristeva Reader*, Oxford: Basil Blackwell.

Moore, B. (1972) *The Catholics*, London: Jonathan Cape.

Morris, J. (1956) *A Ten Year's Anthology*, London: Nonesuch Press.

O'Barr, W. and Atkins, B. (1980) '"Women's language" or "powerless language"?', in S. McConnell-Ginet, R. Borker and N. Furman (eds) *Women and Language in Literature and Society*, New York: Praeger.

Peirce, C.S. (1931–58) *Collected Papers*, Cambridge, Mass.: Harvard University Press.

Peterson, C. and McCabe, A. (1983) *Developmental Psycholinguistics: Three Ways of Looking at Child's Narrative*, New York: Plenum Press.

Polkinghorne, D. (1988) *Narrative Knowing and the Human Sciences*, Albany: SUNY Press.

Ricks, C. (1969) *The Poems of Tennyson*, London: Longman.

Ricks, C. and Michaels, L. (1990) *The State of the Language: 1990s Edition*, London and Boston: Faber & Faber.

Robinson, J.A. and Hawpe, L. (1986) 'Narrative thinking as heuristic process', in T.E. Sarbin (ed.) *Narrative Psychology: the Storied Nature of Human Conduct*, New York: Praeger.

Rothery, J. and Martin, J. (1980) *Writing Project, Papers 1 (Narrative*

Vicarious Experience) and 2 *(Exposition: Literary Criticism)*, Sydney: Department of Linguistics, University of Sydney.

Rumens, C. (1990) *New Women Poets*, Newcastle-upon-Tyne: Bloodaxe Books.

Salzman, E. (1992) 'The tug of history', *The Independent Magazine*, 13 June, 52–8.

Sapir, E. (1921) *Language*, London: Harcourt, Brace & World.

—— (1929) 'The status of linguistics as a science', *Language*, 5: 207–14.

Sarbin, T. (ed.) (1986) *Narrative Psychology: the Storied Nature of Human Conduct*, New York: Praeger.

Scott, L. (1887) *The Life of William Barnes, Poet and Philologist*, London: Macmillan.

Searle, J. (1969) *Speech Acts: an Essay in the Philosophy of Language*, Cambridge: Cambridge University Press.

Shepherd, V. (1990) *Language Variety and the Art of the Everyday*, London: Pinter.

Sheridan, A. (1977) *Jacques Lacan: Ecrits. A Selection Translated from the French*, London: Tavistock.

Short, M. (1992) 'Mind style', *The European English Messenger*, 1 (3): 31–3.

Sisson, C.H. (1965) *Art and Action*, London, Methuen.

Skinner, B.F. (1957) *Verbal Behaviour*, New York: Appleton-Century-Crofts.

Smith, R.D. (1984), *The Writings of Anna Wickham, Free Woman and Poet*, London: Virago Press.

Sontag, S. (1984) *Illness as Metaphor*, Harmondsworth: Penguin.

—— (1990) *AIDS and its Metaphors*, Harmondsworth: Penguin.

Spencer, J. (1986) *The Rise of the Woman Novelist: From Aphra Benn to Jane Austen*, Oxford: Blackwell.

Spender, D. (1980) *Man Made Language*, London: Routledge & Kegan Paul.

Sutcliffe, D. and Wong, A. (eds) (1986) *The Language of the Black Experience*, London: Blackwell.

Sutton-Smith, B. (1986) 'Children's fiction making', in T.R. Sarbin (ed.) *Narrative Psychology: the Storied Nature of Human Conduct*, New York, Praeger.

Swacker, M. (1975) 'The sex of the speaker as a sociolinguistic variable', in B. Thorne and N. Henley (eds) *Language and Sex: Difference and Dominance*, Rowley, Mass.: Newbury House.

Taylor, T.J. (1989) 'Condillac: language as analytic method', *Language and Communication*, 9 (4): 289–97.

Toolan, M. (1988) *Narrative: a Critical Linguistic Introduction*, London and New York: Routledge.

Wells, H.G. (1920), *The Outline of History*, London: Cassell.

Williams, H. (ed.) (1958) *The Poems of Jonathan Swift*, vol. 2, London: Oxford University Press.

Wright, W.A. (1870) 'Provincial glossary', *Notes and Queries*, 12 March: 271.

Wrigley, C. (1984) *William Barnes, the Dorset Poet*, Wimborne: The Dovecote Press.

Zimmerman, D. and West, C. (1975) 'Sex roles, interruptions and silences in conversation', in B. Thorne and N. Henley (eds) *Language and Sex: Difference and Dominance*, Rowley, Mass.: Newbury House, 105–9.

Index